Lifespan Developmental PSYCHOLOGY

DANTES/DSST* Test Study Guide

All rights reserved. This Study Guide, Book and Flashcards are protected under the US Copyright Law. No part of this book or study guide or flashcards may be reproduced, distributed or stored in a retrieval system, or transmitted in any form or by any means, electronic, mechanical, photocopying, recording, or otherwise, without the prior written permission of the publisher Breely Crush Publishing, LLC.

© 2026 Breely Crush Publishing, LLC

DSST is a registered trademark of The Thomson Corporation and its affiliated companies, and does not endorse this book.

971010221143

Copyright ©2003 - 2026, Breely Crush Publishing, LLC.

All rights reserved.

This Study Guide, Book and Flashcards are protected under the US Copyright Law. No part of this publication may be reproduced, distributed or stored in a retrieval system, or transmitted in any form or by any means, electronic, mechanical, photocopying, recording, or otherwise, without the prior written permission of the publisher Breely Crush Publishing, LLC.

Published by Breely Crush Publishing, LLC
10808 River Front Parkway
South Jordan, UT 84095
www.breelycrushpublishing.com

ISBN-10: 1-61433-677-6
ISBN-13: 978-1-61433-677-8

Printed and bound in the United States of America.

DSST is a registered trademark of The Thomson Corporation and its affiliated companies, and does not endorse this book.

Table of Contents

History of Psychology *1*
Mental Health and Behavior *1*
Psychological Approaches *2*
Research Methods *2*
Sexuality *3*
Reproduction *4*
Pregnancy *5*
Development After Birth *9*
Thinking and Perspective *10*
Endocrine System *11*
Genetics *12*
Brain *13*
Right Brain/Left Brain *15*
Memory & Attention *15*
Learning Disabilities *15*
Sight *16*
Hearing *17*
Taste and Smell *17*
Perception *18*
Consciousness *18*
Erikson's Developmental Stages *19*
Jean Piaget *20*
Piaget's Relevant Definitions *21*
Piaget's Stages of Development *22*
Freud's Psychosexual Stages *24*
Id, Ego and Super Ego *25*
Maslow's Hierarchy of Needs *26*
Classical Conditioning *27*
Operant Conditioning *27*
Reinforcers *28*
Defense Mechanisms *28*
Learning Theories *29*
Language Development *31*
Child Learning *33*
Kibbutz *33*
Childhood *33*
Disease *37*
Divorce *37*
Aging *37*

- *Death and Bereavement* *39*
- *Kohlberg's Theory of Moral Development* *40*
- *Morality of Care* *41*
- *Conducting Studies* *42*
- *Sample Test Questions* *48*
- *Test Taking Strategies* *86*
- *Test Preparation* *86*
- *Legal Note* *87*
- *References* *87*

 History of Psychology

Wilhelm Wundt created the first scientific psychology laboratory. In the 16th century, Francis Bacon introduced the scientific method.

 Mental Health and Behavior

Usually mental health and behavior are overlooked on the way to the gym in pursuit of a fit body. But mental health is one of the most important aspects of your well-being to consider in determining your quality of life. **Mental health** is used to describe the thinking part of health. This is just one part of psychosocial health.

Psychosocial health includes:

- Spiritual Health – your thoughts about what gives life purpose – the meaning of life, religion

- Emotional Health – your feelings and reactions

- Mental Health – your thoughts, beliefs, attitudes and values

- Social Health – your interactions with others in social situations

Factors that influence psychosocial health include your family situation, the world around you, life-span and maturity.

Our personality is what makes us unique from other people. It's a dynamic blend of our experiences, heredity, environment and other influences. Our personality determines how we react to problems, stress or other issues.

What is the difference between self-efficacy and self-esteem? Self-efficacy is a term coined by Albert Bandura. It is used to describe a person's belief that they can perform a task successfully, like parenting, attending school or participating in athletics. Self-esteem refers to how much someone values and respects his or herself.

Psychological Approaches

Biological: This theory is based on biology. People who follow this school of thought believe that behavior and personality are linked to their genetics.

Behavioral: The key to this theory is to study and observe behavior. Behaviorists see the individual as a blank slate upon which the impressions of experiences (negative and positive) can be recorded.

Cognitive: Cognitive theorists examine how the mind is involved in knowing, learning, remembering and thinking. They study how the mind relates to behavior.

Humanistic: Humanists believe that all people are inherently good and are motivated to achieve their full potential.

Psychoanalytical: This theory revolves around the individual's unconscious motivation.

Structuralism: Created by Wilhelm Wundt, the name comes from his investigation of the elements or "structures" of the mind. He emphasized the importance of the classification of the mind's structures and focused on conscious thought.

Functionalism: Created by William James, he was interested in the "how" part of behavior. He thought our minds are a continuous flow of information about our experiences. He thought that psychology's role is to study the mind and behavior as they adapt to the environment.

Nature vs. Nurture: Nature means that a child will be born with whatever disposition, tastes, and personality that they were "meant" to have. There are bad seeds. Nurture means that all children are good; it is the way they are brought up that effects their personality and later, their actions. This is an ongoing debate between psychologists.

Research Methods

Experimental research: The experimental method of research is very scientific. This is when a variable and a constant are used to test theories. A **variable** is some changing part of the person that is being studied. Age and gender are variables. A constant is the opposite of a variable.

A **constant** is a factor that always stays the same. In an experiment there is an independent variable and a dependent variable. A **dependent variable** is the variable that the experiment is trying to test or gather information about. An **independent variable** is a variable that the experimenter controls. When an experimenter uses independent and dependent variables, they are exploring the if-then relationship.

Here is an example: **If** you eat a pizza a day (independent variable) **then** you will gain weight (dependent variable). The more precise the hypothesis, the more accurately you can measure the link between the two variables.

Correlational research: Correlational research is used to find the amount that one variable changes in relation to another. For example, is there a correlation between IQ results and grades? Correlation can be positive or negative in results.

Clinical psychologist: Usually has a doctoral degree in psychology plus an internship. They cannot prescribe medicine.

Psychiatrist: A medical doctor with a degree who specializes in psychotherapy. Psychiatrists can prescribe drugs.

Ethics: Principles and standards of behavior, including morals. Determining what is right or wrong and having one's actions correlate with one's beliefs.

 Sexuality

Sexual identity: Recognition of ourselves as sexual beings; a mix of gender identity, gender roles and orientation.

Gonads: The reproductive organs in a male (testes) or females (ovaries).

Puberty: The period of sexual maturation.

Pituitary gland: The gland that controls the release of hormones from the gonads.

Gender: Your sense of being a man or a woman as defined by your society.

Gender roles: Expression of your maleness or femaleness on daily basis.

Gender-role stereotypes: Generalizations about each gender. For example, men are aggressive and more logical. Women are more nurturing and emotional. In the biological sense, androgyny refers to having both male and female sexual characteristics.

However in the field of psychology, androgyny applies to personality traits. In recent times, androgynous personality has begun to be encouraged, as opposed to following gender stereotypes. For example, traditionally women score much lower than men in "dominant" personality traits as women are generally less dominant. Men and women of androgynous personality will score nearly equal, with the men lower than traditional, and the women higher than traditional.

Socialization: Process by which a society identifies its expectations.

Sexual orientation: A person's attraction to other people.

Heterosexual: When a person has an attraction to the opposite sex.

Homosexual: When a person has an attraction to the same sex.

Bisexual: When a person has an attraction to both sexes.

Homophobia: Hatred and or fear of homosexuals.

Celibacy: Not being involved in a sexual relationship.

Autoerotic behavior: Sexual self-stimulation, masturbation.

Erogenous zones: Areas of the body which, when touched, lead to sexual arousal. Four stages of the sexual response:

1. Excitement phase
2. Plateau phase
3. Orgasm phase
4. Resolution phase

Reproduction

Conception is when an ovum or egg is fertilized by sperm. The sperm enters the ovum, leaving the tail outside and securing the area so no other sperm can enter. So, in order for conception to occur, a viable egg, sperm and access to each other are necessary.

Contraception is simply a method to prevent this from happening. The following are different forms of contraception:

- Abstinence – no direct contact with partner's genitals.
- Condom – a sheath of thin latex designed to catch sperm upon ejaculation.
- Oral Contraceptives – "the pill"; a pill designed to prevent pregnancy.
- Spermicides – chemicals meant to kill sperm.
- Diaphragm – small device designed to block access to the uterus. Must be left in place with spermicide for 6-8 hours in order to kill any remaining sperm.
- IUD – T shaped device implanted in the uterus by a physician. This is changed once every five or ten years depending on the type.
- Emergency contraception – drugs taken within three days to prevent pregnancy from instances such as no protection used or a broken condom.
- Depo-Provera – a progesterone (shot) that is given every three months.
- Norplant – a long lasting contraceptive where six capsules are injected in a woman's arm.
- Sterilization – permanent fertility control done through surgical procedures.

If you need more information about any of the previous topics, visit http://www.plannedparenthood.org/

Abortion is the medical means of terminating a pregnancy. RU-486 is a drug that causes an abortion when taken in the first nine weeks of pregnancy.

Pregnancy

When a woman is expecting, they can choose several types of caregivers for their birth process.

- Obstetrician-gynecologist is an M.D. who specializes in obstetrics and gynecology.

- Family practitioner is an M.D. who provides comprehensive care of people of all ages.

- Midwives are experienced practitioners who can attend pregnancies and deliveries.

During a pregnancy, a woman should abstain from all types of drugs. Even over the counter medications such as aspirin and beverages such as coffee and tea can damage a developing fetus.

Teratology is the study of substances which are harmful to prenatal development. These harmful substances are called teratogens. Teratogens are most harmful to the fetus, and include alcohol, tobacco, marijuana, cocaine and other drugs. Diseases such as HIV, AIDS, and rubella are also teratogens. Pollutants like mercury and radiation are all also teratogenic. Although the effects of teratogens are numerous and varied, it is nearly impossible to predict what effects will manifest when a teratogen has been present.

During the embryonic period, growth occurs in two directions. The first is cephalocaudal, or from the head downward. In other words, this means that the head develops faster than the rest of the body. The second type of growth is proximodistal, which is from the center, or spine, outward. This means that the vital organs begin to form before the extremities do.

There are two different types of twins. **Monozygotic twins** are identical twins. **Dizygotic** twins are fraternal twins.

A gene is something that determines physical traits and is inherited from one or both parents. A **zygote** is a fertilized ovum or egg. **Neonate** is another name for newborn. **Prenatal development** is a very critical period, which is the first three months in the womb.

Anoxia is a lack or deficiency of oxygen. This mostly happens during birth itself, by failing to breathe. Cerebral anoxia is more specifically a lack of oxygen to the brain. This can cause permanent damage and is a fairly common problem with infants. Anoxia is a problem in long labors, or if there are complications during birth. Additionally, infants born prematurely or with a very low birth weight have an increased risk of anoxia.

Body cells have 23 pairs. Males have 23 and women have 23 for a grand total of 46 chromosomes.

Klinefelter syndrome occurs when a person has two x chromosomes and one y chromosome, or in other words XXY. Individuals with Klinefelter syndrome have learning disabilities in addition to physical abnormalities. Though the individuals are male, the penis does not grow and breasts may develop. Klinefelter syndrome occurs in approximately 3 of every 1000 males.

Down syndrome is caused by one extra chromosome, for a grand total of 47 chromosomes. To avoid this, parents need to conceive their children at younger ages. A woman's chance of having a Down syndrome baby at age 25 is 1 in 2500; at age 40 the odds are 1 in 100. Men over 55 also have a higher rate of fathering Down syndrome children. Down syndrome is where the child has one extra chromosome, which is number 21.

Mentally retarded is defined as a low IQ and a mental age of about 4 years old. Of all health problems, those who are mentally retarded are the **least likely to have cerebral palsy as well.**

Autism is a lack of responsiveness to other people. Autism is rare in children of either sex in the first 2 ½ years. At birth, cells in the cerebral cortex are not well connected. They are lacking in myelin, which is insulation for nerves.

Rubella is a disease, also called German measles.

Critical period is a specific period in development when a certain event will have the greatest impact. For example, a certain species of bird has a certain period of time when their young can learn to fly. If they do not learn during that time, then they will never learn to fly.

Fetal alcohol syndrome is when babies have been in the womb when the mother was consuming alcohol. The problems include slowed growth, body and face malfunctions, nervous system disorders and mental retardation. Fetal Alcohol Syndrome, or FAS, is the severe end of a spectrum of effects that can occur when a woman drinks during pregnancy. Fetal death is the most extreme outcome. There is no known safe amount of alcohol to drink while pregnant and there also does not appear to be a safe time to drink during pregnancy either. Therefore, it is recommended that women abstain from drinking alcohol at any time during pregnancy. The first trimester of a pregnancy is the most dangerous for the fetus in regard to alcohol or drug use. Some of the problems which characterize FAS are small stature in relation to peers, poor coordination, hyperactive behavior, learning disabilities, mental retardation or low IQ, and having a large head.

Fetal tobacco syndrome is what a baby can get if their mother smokes while pregnant. Five cigarettes are too many; the child will have problems, with a 50% greater risk of getting childhood cancer. The baby can also be born with a low birth weight.

Amniocentesis is when a sample is taken from the fluid in the amnionic sac to be tested for various diseases or genetic traits.

For those giving birth, **medicated delivery** is the most popular. Dr. Grantly Dick Read started teaching natural prepared childbirth. **Gentle birth** is when the baby is born in a pool or bath with dim lights. **Cesarean birth** is a surgical delivery.

Fontanels are areas in a baby's skull where cartilage has not yet hardened into bone. These soft spots allow the plates of bone that form the skull to shift or flex, making childbirth easier. There are two fontanels, the anterior fontanel at the front of the head and the posterior fontanel farther back. Generally, the posterior fontanel will harden within two months of the child's birth, while the anterior fontanel will not harden until the child is two.

Rh factor has to do with your blood. If you are A positive, you are Rh positive. If a husband and wife have different blood types, then it can cause a problem for the baby. If the baby has Rh-positive blood and the mother is Rh negative it could cause the mother's cells to attack the baby. To fix this, injections are given in the doctor's office or hospital.

If a child cannot be conceived via the usual method, this is called infertility. There are now several alternatives including:

- Alternative (also known as artificial) insemination: depositing the semen into the body via a thin tube in a doctor's office.
- In vitro fertilization: fertilization of the egg done outside the body and then the egg is transferred back into the body.

Ferdinand Lamaze taught women breathing procedures to get through childbirth. This includes panting.

Growth of the brain is not complete at birth. The cerebral cortex is the least developed part of a newborn.

Stillbirth is medical term for the birth of a dead baby.

Sudden Infant Death Syndrome (SIDS) the death of a child under 1 year for no apparent reason. Physicians do not know what causes this to happen but recommend putting babies on their backs to sleep and not to have anything extra, toys, pillows or blankets, in the bed or crib. Also, do not sleep with a baby in your bed.

STDs are Sexually Transmitted Diseases which include AIDS and Herpes.

Toxic Shock Syndrome (TSS) is a sometimes fatal disease that can occur with the excessive use of tampons as well as leaving a diaphragm inside longer than prescribed (no longer than 8 hours after insertion).

Syphilis and rubella are two diseases which can be very dangerous to the fetus. Both diseases are most dangerous to the fetus when caught early in the pregnancy. Often, syphilis causes miscarriages or stillbirths. It is possible for the infant to catch the disease during birth. If a mother catches rubella in the first trimester, there is a ninety percent chance that the fetus will be affected. It can cause miscarriage, stillbirths, heart defects, deafness, and other problems. It is very important that both of these diseases are avoided during pregnancy.

Development After Birth

Neonates have senses. This means that you can startle them in the womb with a loud noise. Their hearing is mostly developed. Eyes are not fully developed when babies are first born. They can distinguish color very early in their development. Newborns (neonates) can track movement and bright objects.

Doctors agree that breast-feeding is the best way to feed your baby.

The "Virginia Apgar" sometimes referred to as the "Apgar Rating" is what doctors use to judge a baby when it is first born. It is rated on the following areas, getting a score of 0-2 in each area:

- Appearance
- Pulse
- Grimace (reflex, irritability)
- Activity
- Respiration

Infants have the capacity to learn. **Habituation**, a simple type of learning, is to get used to something. Some people live near trains. When a train goes by your house every day, and in the night while you are asleep, it is easy to stop hearing the train. You become used to the noise and it does not bother you.

PKU is an enzyme deficiency. 1 in 14,000 will get it and will become mentally retarded if they do not receive treatment. They are tested in the first 3-6 weeks of life. PKU is short for **phenylketonuria.**

The **Visual Cliff** shows that infants have depth perception. This is a study that was done by having infants placed on a solid, opaque surface. The infant's mothers were placed at the end of the table, where the opaque surface disappeared and glass began. The infants did not want to cross the glass because they could see the distance between where they were and the floor.

Temperament in infants is measured by monitoring:

- Irritability
- Social responsiveness
- Activity level

Object permanence is developed around age two. This means that a child will understand that once you leave the room, you are not gone forever. If you go around a corner, out of their vision, they know you are just around the corner.

According to the psychoanalytic theory, infants develop a secure attachment when a parent pays attention to, and responds appropriately to, the needs of the child. This is critical for the emotional development and security of a child.

Harry Harlow did an experiment with baby monkeys about affection and love. He took baby monkeys away from their mothers while they were still nursing and gave them two pretend monkeys in their cage. One was made of wire and had a bottle. The other was made of cloth but did not have a bottle. The monkeys preferred the one with cloth so much that they clung to it, only interacting with the wire monkey for food.

Thinking and Perspective

There are many difficulties in measuring intelligence. Alfred Binet made the first IQ test. IQ tests are not a good indicator for children over a long period of time. It is possible to be coached in learning a particular type of question or test and have the score improve dramatically. IQ=Mental age divided by chronological age multiplied by 100.

$$IQ = MA/CA \times 100$$

IQ scores are only accurate for a short period of time. They measure a child against their peers.

Hyperactivity only affects **three percent** of all children. They have a short attention span.

Creative people are mostly **divergent** thinkers; this would include *gifted* or advanced children. **Divergent** thinking is a creative process. **Convergent** thinking is follower thinking.

Divergent thinking is a process in which many ideas are brainstormed to explore many possible solutions. In other words, divergent thinking could be considered thinking creatively. Studies have shown that the ability to use divergent thinking is not related to IQ level, but to personality traits such as persistence, curiosity, and nonconformity.

Convergent thinking is a process by which a particular set of steps is followed to come to a correct answer. Mathematic and scientific procedures require convergent thinking.

This is the type of thought which is generally used in academic settings, as opposed to divergent thinking which is used in creative settings.

Dialectical perspective is a thought process which considers an idea or belief, which is called a thesis, and acknowledges the opposite of that idea, which is called the antithesis. These two levels are then considered and a synthesis is created which forges the two together. The simplest way to state it is that a person who uses dialectical perspective has a stated position, but also acknowledges that it may change with time.

Cross-modal perception is the ability to associate something from one area of knowledge, such as what it looks like, tastes like or feels like, and use that the determine or imagine what it is like in other aspects. For example, many infants like to put things in their mouth. By doing this, they most directly learn what it tastes or feels like, but they may also learn what, in general, it looks like. Studies have shown that even infants two months old when given the chance to hold an object, and are then shown two objects, will recognize the object they held. This is cross-modal perception.

Raymond Cattell proposed the idea that different types of intellectual pursuits could be classified as one of two types. They are fluid intelligence and crystallized intelligence. Fluid intelligence is the type of thought related to numerical and intellectual puzzles, quick and creative responses. Crystallized intelligence is anything which has to do with factual information. Crystallized intelligence includes trivia, vocabulary, scientific principles, and historical dates.

Nature vs. Nurture is an old debate between two schools of thought. Nature means that a child will be born with whatever disposition, tastes and personality they were "meant" to have. Those who believe in the nature theory think that there are bad seeds. Those who ascribe to the nurture view believe that all children are good. They believe it is the way they are brought up that affects their personality and later, their actions.

Separated at birth, identical twins were studied and found later to have very similar jobs, haircuts, styles of dressing, etc. This shows that heredity has an impact. What does this study support? Nature or nurture? (Nature).

 Endocrine System

The endocrine system is made up of the **hypothalamus** and other endocrine glands. Endocrine glands create and release chemicals into the bloodstream. The **pituitary gland** releases hormones that regulate the hormone secretions of other glands. The pituitary gland is located at the base of the skull and is about the size of a pea. Adrenal glands affect our moods, energy level and stress. Adrenal glands also secrete epinephrine (adrenaline) and norepinephrine.

The nervous system has an area called the **Autonomic Nervous System (ANS).** ANS works as an involuntary system; usually, we don't know it is there. Other involuntary systems include respiratory and cardiac functions. Here's the test: if you have to think about doing it, it's not involuntary. ANS is most important in the "fight or flight" response. When we experience large amounts of stress such as in an emergency, our body gives us extra energy (adrenaline) to fight, perhaps against an attacker, or to take flight, to run from the attacker. In non-stress times, this system allows us to rest and digest. This system is broken up into three different areas. These are:

- **Sympathetic nervous system**: arousing part of the system
- **Parasympathetic nervous system**: calming part of the system
- Enteric nervous system

Limbic system: Structures in the cerebral cortex related to memory and emotion.

Hippocampus: Located in the limbic system. Its primary function is to store memories.

Cerebral cortex: The most developed part of the brain. Largest part of the brain (80%). Underneath the cerebral cortex are four lobes of the brain. These are:

- Occipital lobe: related to vision
- Temporal lobe: hearing
- Frontal lobe: voluntary muscles and intelligence
- Parietal lobe: body sensations

Genetics

Gregor Mendel was the father of genetics and inheritance. He was a priest in charge of a garden who got interested in some of the plants. Pea pods are self-fertilizing. Three of four seeds were purple; one seed out of four was white. Each plant contained two genetic codes. The purple was dominant over white because it showed up more often. Look at the chart below to determine the chances of getting each kind of plant:

PP=Purple (Upper case means dominant, lower case means recessive)
pp=White

	Purple	White
Purple	PP	P*p*
White	*p*P	*pp*

The inheritance of sex is determined by the x and the y chromosome. All chromosomes come in pairs. For use in the chart, females are XX and males are XY.

	X	X
X	XX	XX
Y	YX	YX

To get the values (YX), all you do is add the intersection of each row and column on the table. According to the table above (and biology) the chances of having either a boy or girl are 50%.

Chromosomes in DNA carry genes.

In a **somatic cell** there is a full set of chromosomes (there is a total of 46 chromosomes, thus 46 genes). Cloning is done by creating reproduction using only the somatic cell.

Gametes are the reproductive cells (eggs and sperm). Each has exactly one-half a set of normal chromosomes; this is why you need one of each to conceive. Gametes fuse together to make a zygote. A zygote is the first part of a human. Only a few genes are on the "y" chromosome. All genes on the "y" are passed on to boys every time, but never to girls.

Brain

The brain is a part of the central nervous system. It controls all necessary functions of the body. All emotions originate in the brain as well as memory and thought processes. It interprets signals from other parts of the body and turns those signals into rational thought such as, "My leg hurts from running too much." This developed brain is what makes us human by controlling our emotions, thoughts and consciousness.

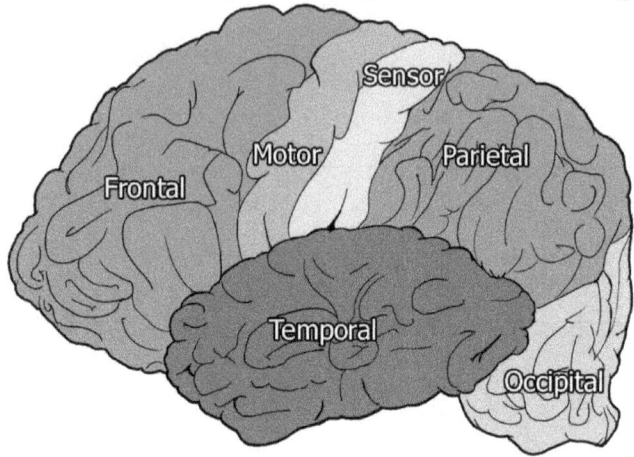

The brain is located in the skull. The skull protects this organ. There are also other things that protect the brain. There are three membranes that shield it. The outer layer, the dura mater, is the strongest and thickest. Beneath that layer is another membrane, called the arachnoid layer. Beneath that, the final layer is the pia mater, which is mostly blood vessels. A clear fluid called cerebrospinal fluid covers the entire brain and is used to transport chemicals through the brain and to regulate pressure.

The brain and the spinal cord make up the central nervous system. The Cerebrum is the two large halves of the brain that you can see on the left. The deep "crack" in the middle is called the longitudinal fissure. The two halves of the brain communicate via bundles of axons called commissures. The largest commissure is called the corpus callosum.

Cerebrum: Houses memories and controls our responses to different sensory signals.

Cerebellum: Coordinates all movements and muscles.

Pons: Control breathing and heart rate.

Brain stem: Sends commands to all other parts of the body.

Thalamus: Main relay station for incoming sensory signals to cerebral cortex and outgoing motor signals from it. All the senses but **smell** report to the thalamus.

Hypothalamus: Regulates internal temperature, eating, sleeping, drinking, emotions, and sexual activity.

Right Brain/Left Brain

Many people think that if you are "left brained" then you have a higher aptitude in math and science, as thinking is supposedly more analytical in that area. The "right" half of the brain is supposedly where creativity and art come from. This is a myth. Something important you need to know is the left half of the brain controls the right hand, right eye, and speech. The right half of the brain controls the left hand, left eye and simple comprehension.

Memory & Attention

Memory is made up of three parts: encoding the information; representation of the information; and retrieving of what was previously stored in memory. As we age, sometimes the ability to recall information is reduced. This has nothing to do with the level of intelligence or education of the individual. As a person ages, their short term memory can become incapacitated. **Selective attention** is focusing attention on a small amount of information. Attention can be selective just like hearing. Sometimes it is hard to hear or pay attention to ideas or thoughts that don't resonate with our goals or actions.

Learning Disabilities

When children do not perform well in school, sometimes it can be attributed to a hearing loss, vision loss or learning disability. One of the most common learning disabilities is dyslexia which is a disability in reading. Another learning disability is dyscalcula which is a math disability where concepts are learned one day and forgotten the next, including simple 12 + 3 equations. There is not a specific cause for a learning disability but most people believe it to be organic or biochemical.

Although not a learning disability, ADD (Attention Deficit Disorder) and ADHD (Attention Hyper Deficit Disorder) interfere with the learning process.

ADHD, or Attention-Deficit Hyperactivity Disorder, is a type of learning disability in which a person has difficulty concentrating. They may be easily distracted, feel the need to be constantly in motion, or just inattentive. Diagnosing ADHD is difficult because there are a number of possible causes, and it is partially subjective. There is evidence which shows that ADHD can be genetic or caused by lead poisoning, vitamin deficiencies, or be a product of a stressful environment. ADHD cannot be diagnosed using an

MRI or other type of brain scan, though often for research purposes MRIs of normal and ADHD children are compared. Generally, diagnosis requires up to six months of observation, and information gathering by doctors.

 Sight

The vestibular sense is the sense that gives information about balance and body movement. It tells you if your body is moving, tilting, shaking, etc.

Absolute threshold: How much sensation do you have to experience to feel a feather brush your skin? Each person has an absolute threshold that is the minimum amount of something we can detect or sense.

Sclera: White part of the eye that protects and manages the shape of the eye.

Iris: Ring of muscles that make up the colored part of the eye.

Pupil: The part of the eye that looks black is the opening of the iris. It opens and closes to let the correct amount of light enter the eye.

Cornea: A clear membrane in front of the eye that protects it.

Lens: It is transparent and is located in the front of the eye.

The cornea and the lens are responsible for bending the light falling on the eye and focusing it in the back of the eye. To help the eye focus, the lens changes its curves. This process is called **accommodation.**

The **retina** is in the back of the eye and is light sensitive. It includes receptors called cones and rods and other neurons. Receptors are important for the ability to see. Rods (each is a receptor) are very sensitive to light but do not help with color vision. Cones are what we use to view colors. There are three types of cones used to determine colors by comparing the results between the three cones. There is only one type of rod so it is not helpful in determining color, as it has nothing to compare to.

Hearing

The Auditory System is another term for hearing. Sound is another way that we get information about our environment. Sounds or sound waves are vibrations in the air that we receive through the ear and are processed by our hearing system.

Noise: Irrelevant stimuli that compete for our attention (traffic, for example).

Frequency: The number of full wavelengths that pass through a point in a given amount of time.

Pitch: The ear's interpretation of a sound's frequency (e.g., notes in a musical song).

Amplitude: Amplitude is the amount of pressure produced by a sound wave and is measured in dB or decibels.

Loudness: A sound wave's amplitude.

Timbre: The tone color or perceptual quality of a sound.

Outer ear: Includes the pinna and the external auditory canal.

Middle ear: Area of the ear with three main parts, eardrum, anvil and stirrup.

Inner ear: Oval window, cochlea, organ of Corti.

Cochlea: A fluid-filled structure in the inner ear that looks like a snail.

Organ of corti: A part of the ear inside the cochlea. Contains sensors that change energy into impulses that are decoded by the brain.

Taste and Smell

Taste is an important sense. On top of the tongue are papillae that are bumps that contain the taste buds. The taste buds recognize taste in four areas that are sweet, bitter, salty, and sour.

Smell is also an important sense. Smell can trigger emotion and memories. The scientific name for the sense of smell is the olfactory sense. A person can smell something, like food, when airborne molecules of an odor reach tiny receptor cells in the nasal cavity. The olfactory epithelium, located at the top of the nasal cavity, is where the receptor cells are located for smell. These receptor cells have hair-like antennae that make contact with the air, which help us smell.

Perception

Perception is the way that the brain organizes and gives meaning to the information provided by the senses. Perception processes have four characteristics that are:

- Automatic: you do not have to think about it. It happens automatically.
- Selective: you may be more interested in a cute boy rather than what he is saying.
- Contextual: perception is contextual. If you have heard a movie is scary, you may be more inclined to get scared.
- Creative: perception fills in areas that we do not have complete information about. For example, when a friend's face is partially blocked by their hair, your mind fills in the blanks about how their face looks underneath the hair.

Gestalt psychology is an approach that assumes that people organize their perceptions by patterns. They believe in the principle of closure. When someone sees an incomplete form, they fill in the pieces.

Your eyes and mind interpret this to be a triangle, when in fact, it is just a line. This is an example of the principle of closure.

Depth perception is what makes a person able to see objects as they are, in three dimensions. It is what causes some items to look farther away or close up. We see depth by using two kinds of cues. These cues are called binocular cues and monocular cues. Binocular cues are cues made with both eyes. Monocular cues are made by each eye working alone.

Consciousness

Consciousness is an awareness. This includes an awareness of external events, which are things that happen outside of your body. Internal events are things that happen inside your body such as internal thoughts about your emotions and body functions. William James thought of the mind as a stream of consciousness, a flow of emotions, sensations and thoughts. Contrastingly, Freud believed the unconscious motivates our actions (through the id, ego and superego).

Sometimes we have daydreams. Daydreaming is another form of consciousness that involves very little effort. It is like dreaming while we are awake. Letting your mind wander is a form of daydreaming.

When people take drugs, their mind is in an altered state of consciousness. Other states of consciousness include meditation, trauma, hypnosis, fatigue, etc.

Erikson's Developmental Stages

Erik Erikson was a psychoanalyst who documented stages of emotional growth in regards to human babies. Each stage has different needs and lessons to be learned. If the child or infant does not learn a specific lesson, he may have a harder time in life down the road. For example, if a baby is crying constantly and is not taken care of, or if they are ignored, they can come to feel mistrust towards others. Another example is found in the young adult stage. The young adult must deal with either being intimate with someone or dealing with feeling isolated. According to Erikson, the most important development is the development of trust.

Infant *Trust vs. Mistrust*
Infants gain trust and confidence from their caregivers. If those caregivers are warm and responsive then they will know that the world is good. Mistrust occurs from being handled poorly and inattentiveness on the part of the caregiver.

Toddler *Autonomy vs. Shame and Doubt*
Children want to make their own decisions. Autonomy is when the parents give the child that necessary free rein over their choices.

Preschooler *Initiative vs. Guilt*
Children play at different roles. They can try their hand at being a princess or a mother or father to their dolls. Ever wonder why children at this age love dress-up clothes?

School-Age Child *Industry vs. Inferiority*
Children learn to work with others.

Adolescent *Identity vs. Role Confusion*
This is the standard teen question: "Who am I?"

Young Adult   *Intimacy vs. Isolation*
Young adults seek emotional ties with others. Because of earlier trust situations (divorce of parents, for example), some young adults are unable to form attachments and this leaves them isolated.

Middle-Age Adult   *Generativity vs. Stagnation*
Generativity means giving to the next generation. Those that do not do these things feel unhappy.

Old Age   *Ego Integrity vs. Despair*
In this stage, people think about what they have done with their life. Integrity comes from achieving what one wanted in life. Despair results in fear of death for those that are unhappy with their past.

Jean Piaget

Jean Piaget (1896-1980) was a biologist who originally studied mollusks (publishing twenty scientific papers on them by the time he was 21) but moved into the study of the development of children's understanding, through observing them and talking and listening to them while they worked on exercises he set.

His view of how children's minds work and develop has been enormously influential, particularly in educational theory. His particular insight was the role of maturation (simply growing up) in children's increasing capacity to understand their world: they cannot undertake certain tasks until they are psychologically mature enough to do so. His research has spawned a great deal more, much of which has undermined the details of his own, but like many other investigators, his importance comes from his overall vision.

He proposed that children's thinking does not develop entirely smoothly; instead, there are certain points at which it 'takes off' and moves into completely new areas and capabilities. He saw these transitions as taking place at about 18 months, 7 years and 11 or 12 years. This has been taken to mean that before these ages children are not capable (no matter how bright) of understanding things in certain ways, and that theory has been used as the basis for scheduling the school curriculum.[a] Piaget is a **cognitive theorist.** Piaget believed that the individual actively constructs knowledge about the world.

 Piaget's Relevant Definitions

Adolescent Egocentrism: When adolescents truly believe themselves to be "the center of the universe" to those around them. This can lead them to believe that no one else has ever had the same experiences as they have, i.e., no one has ever felt this badly or been this misunderstood. This is a theory of David Elkind, who agrees with Piaget's theories.

Assimilation: The process by which a person takes material into their mind from the environment, which may mean changing the evidence of their senses to make it fit.

Accommodation: The difference made to one's mind or one's concepts by the process of assimilation. Note that assimilation and accommodation go together; you can't have one without the other.

Classification: The ability to group objects together on the basis of common features.

Class Inclusion: The understanding of more advanced than simple classification, that some classes or sets of objects are also sub-sets of a larger class. (e.g. There is a class of objects called dogs. There is also a class called animals. But all dogs are also animals, so the class of animals includes that of dogs.)

Conservation: The realization that objects or sets of objects stay the same even when they are changed about or made to look different. For example, children can understand that the same amount of liquid is in two differently shaped jars.

Developmental Norm: A statistical measure of typical scores for categories of information.

Egocentrism: The belief that you are the center of the universe and everything revolves around you, and the corresponding inability to see the world as someone else does and adapt to it. Not moral "selfishness," just an early stage of psychological development. The move away from egocentrism is called decentration.

Elaboration: Relating new information to something familiar. An example would be learning how to cook a pasta dish. You may have cooked something similar in the past. In your mind your may think, "This is like that time I made spaghetti except now I do…"

Equilibrium: A state of mental balance, reconciling new experiences with new understanding.

Invincibility Fable: The elated feeling adolescents have, that they are immune to risks, mortality and probability. This leads them into risky actions, with a false sense of security thinking they will never fall, get killed or get caught. This term was also coined by David Elkind.

Operation: The process of working something out in your head. Young children (in the sensorimotor and pre-operational stages) have to act, and try things out in the real world, to work things out (like count on fingers); older children and adults can do more in their heads, mentally.

Recognition: Is the ability to identify correctly something encountered before.

Recall: Is being able to reproduce knowledge from memory.

Schema (or scheme): The representation in the mind of a set of perceptions, ideas, and/or actions, which go together.

Stage: A period in a child's development in which he or she is capable of understanding some things but not others

Piaget's Stages of Development

This table was created by James Atherton and defines the different developmental stages according to Jean Piaget.[b]

Developmental Stage and Approximate Age	Characteristic Behavior
Sensory Motor Period (0-24 months)	
Reflexive Stage (0-2 months)	Simple reflex activity such as grasping and sucking.
Primary Circular Reactions (2-4 months)	Reflexive behaviors occur in stereotyped repetition such as opening and closing fingers repetitively.
Secondary Circular Reactions (4-8 months)	Repetition of actions to reproduce interesting consequences such as kicking one's feet to move a mobile suspended over the crib.

Coordination of Secondary Reactions (8-12 months)	Responses become coordinated into more complex sequences. Actions take on an "intentional" character such as the infant reaches behind a screen to obtain a hidden object.
Tertiary Circular Reactions (12-18 months)	Discovery of new ways to produce the same consequence or obtain the same goal such as the infant pulling a pillow toward him in an attempt to get a toy resting on it.
Invention of New Means Through Mental Combination (18-24 months)	Evidence of an internal representational system. Symbolizing the problem-solving sequence before actually responding. Deferred imitation.
The Preoperational Period (2-7 years)	
Preoperational Phase (2-4 years)	Increased use of verbal representation but speech is egocentric. The beginnings of symbolic rather than simple motor play. Transductive reasoning. Can think about something without the object being present by use of language.
Intuitive Phase (4-7 years)	Speech becomes more social, less egocentric. The child has an intuitive grasp of logical concepts in some areas. However, there is still a tendency to focus attention on one aspect of an object while ignoring others. Concepts formed are crude and irreversible. Easy to believe in magical increase, decrease, disappearance. Reality not firm. Perceptions dominate judgment. In the moral-ethical realm, the child is not able to show principles underlying best behavior. Rules of a game cannot develop in the mind; only uses simple do's and do not's imposed by authority.

Period of Concrete Operations (7-11 years)
Evidence for organized, logical thought. There is the ability to perform multiple classification tasks, order objects in a logical sequence, and comprehend the principle of conservation. Thinking becomes less transductive and less egocentric. The child is capable of concrete problem solving. Some reversibility now possible (quantities moved can be restored such as in arithmetic: 3+4 = 7 and 7-4 = 3, etc.) Classifying logic-finding bases to sort unlike objects into logical groups where previously it was on superficial perceived attributes such as color. Categorical labels such as "number" or animal" now available.
Period of Formal Operations (11-15 years)
Thought becomes more abstract, incorporating the principles of formal logic. The ability to generate abstract propositions, multiple hypotheses and their possible outcomes is evident. Thinking becomes less tied to concrete reality. Formal logical systems can be acquired. Can handle proportions, algebraic manipulation, and other purely abstract processes. If a + b = x then x = a b. If ma/ca = IQ = 1.00 then Ma = CA. Prepositional logic present, in as-if and if-then steps. Can use aids such as axioms to transcend human limits on comprehension. Can think hypothetically and test hypothesis. Based on the information in these stages, you can see it is important to have age appropriate materials in school.

Piaget and Freud both agreed that environmental influences could affect the time spent in stages but not the order.

 # Freud's Psychosexual Stages

Stage	Age	Description
Oral	Birth-1 year	The new ego directs the baby's sucking activities toward breast or bottle. If oral needs are not met appropriately, the individual may develop such habits as thumb sucking, fingernail biting, pencil chewing, overeating and smoking.
Anal	1-3 Years	Young toddlers and preschoolers enjoy holding and releasing urine and feces. Toilet training becomes a major issue between parent and child. If parents insist that children be trained before they are ready or make too few demands, conflicts about anal control may appear in the form of extreme orderliness and cleanliness or messiness and disorder.

Phallic	3-6 Years	Id impulses transfer to the genitals, and the child finds pleasure in genital stimulation. Freud's Oedipus Conflict for boys and Electra Conflict for girls take place. Young children feel a sexual desire for the other-sex parent. To avoid punishment, they give up this desire and instead adopt the same-sex parent's characteristics and values. As a result, the superego is formed and children feel guilty each time they violate its standards. The relationships between id, ego and superego established at this time determine the individual's basic personality orientation.
Latency	6-11 years	Sexual instincts die down, and the superego develops further. The child acquires new social values from adults outside the family and from play with same-sex peers.
Genital	Adolescence	Puberty causes the sexual impulses of the phallic stage to reappear. If development has been successful during earlier stages, it leads to marriage, mature sexuality, and the birth and rearing of children.

Id, Ego and Super Ego

Sigmund Freud's analysis of human personality and subconscious drives features three main components id, ego, and superego. Together, these mechanisms combine to aide us in our decision-making and guide us to become the unique individuals that we all are. Robert Young, a professor with expertise in this area, provided the following information used to understand the id, superego and the ego.

<u>*The id*</u> contains the psychic content related to the primitive instincts of the body, notably sex and aggression, as well as all psychic material that is inherited and present at birth. It functions entirely according to the pleasure-pain principle, its impulses either seeking immediate fulfillment or settling for a compromise fulfillment.

<u>*The superego*</u> is the ethical component of the personality and provides the moral standards by which the ego operates.

<u>*The ego*</u> coexists, in psychoanalytic theory; with the id and superego...it is the integrator between the outer and inner worlds, as well as between the id and the superego. The ego gives continuity and consistency to behavior by providing a personal point of reference, which relates the events of the past (retained in memory) and actions of the present and of the future (represented in anticipation and imagination).
(SOURCE: Britannica.com)

The main trio of characters found in Star Trek, the original series McCoy, Kirk, and Spock makes for an interesting analogy of human personality as they each show characteristics of Freud's concepts of the id, ego, and superego. Hopefully, this analogy will make it easier for you to understand and remember this theory.

THE ID James T. Kirk, always enjoyed a good fight, risked his ship and crew often, and always fed his libido with an assortment of females. Kirk, with his passion for gratification in terms of aggression and sex, displays characteristics of the id.

THE SUPEREGO Doctor Leonard (Bones) McCoy, always reminded his Captain of the rules and morality of any situation. He also is known for his arguments with Spock, just as the superego and ego are often in conflict.

THE EGO Mr. Spock was the bringer of balance between the impulses of the id and the extreme caution of the superego by his use of logic and understanding of his Captain's needs as well as understanding the morality base of Bones. While Spock and Bones were often at odds, they always worked toward the same end a correct and feasible solution to any given situation.

Together Kirk, McCoy, and Spock represent the triadic conflict within all humans, thus the three distinct characters, taken together, form an understanding of the human condition.[c]

Maslow's Hierarchy of Needs

Maslow's Hierarchy of Needs consists of the following stages from the top down:

- Self-actualization
- Esteem needs
- Belonging and love
- Safety
- Physical needs

These stages begin at physical needs. First you need to have food, water, and shelter before you can worry about other requirements. Once those needs are met you may start to think of other necessities, such as safety. You might buy a gun or move to a more prosperous and safe area. Once you are fed, clothed and safe you will want to meet needs of belonging and love through relationships. If you feel loved, you may begin to think about your self-esteem and how you feel as a person, what you are contributing. The final stage, self-actualization, you may never meet. Most people do not.

Carl Rogers agreed with Maslow's Hierarchy of Needs and was a true advocate of group therapy. He believed that each person had an idea of a "perfect person" and tried to work towards being like that person as much as possible. He believed that people needed to become "fully functioning" individuals. Rogers and Maslow were both Humanistic Theorists.

Classical Conditioning

The first scientific experiment of classical conditioning was done by a Russian scientist named Ivan Pavlov. In Pavlov's famous dog experiment, he would ring a bell and then feed the dogs. Initially, the dogs would salivate when given food. Over time, the dogs began to salivate at the sound of the bell. Classical conditioning describes a link between a stimulus and a response in which a person or animal associates or substitutes a neutral stimulus, such as the bell, with the actual stimulus, the food. Many reflexive reactions, such as a person covering their eyes when something flies in front of their face, or salivating at the smell of their favorite food, can be explained through classical conditioning.

Operant Conditioning

Operant conditioning is a type of conditioning in which a person associates an action with a consequence. The main difference between operant conditioning and classical conditioning is that classical conditioning works more to explain reflexive or unconscious reactions, whereas operant conditioning works to explain elective actions and reactions. For example, a student will wish to do well in school because it brings the consequence of good grades and parental approval. Studies have shown that even infants can be taught certain behaviors using operant conditioning. The name most associated with operant conditioning is B. F. Skinner.

The Premack principle is a system which uses operant conditioning to make less probable actions more likely to occur by using more probable actions as reinforcers. For example, most children do not like doing laundry, making it the less probable action. However, most children do enjoy watching television, making it the more probable action. If a mother tells her children that they can watch television if they do the laundry, she is using the Premack principle, with the television being the reinforcer.

Reinforcers

Operant conditioning depends upon reinforcers as a method of learning. A reinforcer is anything which makes a behavior more likely to reoccur. Reinforcers can be positive or negative. A positive reinforcer is when something pleasant is used to make a behavior more likely. Parents paying their children for good grades or a person giving their pet a treat for doing a trick are both examples of positive reinforcers. A negative reinforcer is when something unpleasant is removed from a situation. For example, if a student studies more, they are less anxious. The anxiety is an unpleasant feeling which is removed as a result of studying, and therefore studying is a form of negative reinforcement. Conditioning can also occur using punishments, which instead of making a behavior more likely to reoccur, attempt to make it less likely to reoccur. Like reinforcers, punishments can be both positive and negative.

In addition to being positive and negative, reinforcers can also be described as extrinsic or intrinsic. An extrinsic reinforcer is something physical (tangible), or from the environment. Payment for work, a treat for doing well, and earning a prize for winning a game are all extrinsic reinforcers. An intrinsic reinforcer, on the other hand, is something which comes from within the individual, or in other words, something emotional. Self-satisfaction or the happiness which comes from praise are intrinsic reinforcers. The values of extrinsic and intrinsic reinforcers are different for everyone.

Defense Mechanisms

Defense mechanisms are developed to help us relieve stress. We can choose to accept, deny or change our perceptions and feelings to be in harmony with our values. Here is a list of the most common defense mechanisms and what they mean:

Denial: Complete rejection of the feeling or situation.

Suppression: Hiding the feelings and not acknowledging them.

Reaction Formation: Turning a feeling into the exact opposite feeling. For example, saying you hate someone you are interested in.

Projection: Projection is transferring your thoughts and feelings onto others. For example, someone who is being unfaithful themselves constantly accuses their partner of cheating.

Displacement: Feelings are redirected to someone else. Someone who has a bad day at work and can't complain goes home and yells at their kids instead.

Rationalization: You deny your feelings and come up with ways to justify your behavior.

Regression: Reverting to old behavior to avoid feelings.

Sublimation: A type of displacement, a redirection of the feeling into a socially productive activity.

Learning Theories

John B Watson argued that if psychology was a true science, then psychologists should only study what they could see and measure. Behaviorism, now also called learning theory, is based on the principle of observing and correcting behavior.

A Russian Scientist named Ivan Pavlov did a study between stimulus and response. This study most commonly referred to as Pavlov's Dogs, when Pavlov discovered Classical Conditioning.

Pavlov was researching salivation in dogs. He realized that the dogs began to salivate not only at the sight of food but eventually, at the sound of the footsteps of the attendants that were bringing the food. This observation led him through classical conditioning to make a dog salivate when a bell was heard.

Pavlov began by ringing the bell just before feeding the dog and created through several steps salivation by only hearing the sound of the bell. Classical conditioning is when an animal or person responds to a neutral stimulus (like the bell) with a meaningful one (food).

Skinner was one of the most important learning theorists of our time. Skinner agreed that classical conditioning explains some types of behaviors, but he believed that operant conditioning played a much larger role. Operant conditioning teaches that when a certain action is performed, there are consequences. Operant conditioning reinforces good behavior. You can teach your dog to fetch your slippers by teaching him the action and then giving him a reward. It can be said that all social interactions are a result of operant conditioning, i.e., getting peer approval for your new car or earning a paycheck. Reinforcement is the term for the positive or useful consequence to an action. An intrinsic reinforcer is something that comes from inside the individual, like satisfaction for doing a good job. An extrinsic reinforcer is anything outside yourself, in the environment that reinforces your behavior, such as getting good grades, resulting in a scholarship or discounts on insurance.

Instructional conditioning gives a negative sanction. Extinction is done best gradually through shaping. Extinction is the process of unassociating the condition with the response. When you ring the bell for your cat to get dinner and then don't provide him with any food, gradually the cat will learn not to come when the bell is sounded. Response extinction is a method of modifying behavior. It ignores the behavior so you don't have the response.

Egocentric behavior means that a child does not take into consideration other people's needs. This is especially important in divorce when the child is in this stage. The child is incapable of understanding that he or she is not the result of the breakup because to that child, the world revolves around them. Children in their preschool years tend to have an egocentric view of the world, in other words thinking centers around the ego or self. This "self-centered" view does not necessarily mean selfish. Egocentric means that the child's perceptions are limited to their own point of view. A child who sees someone crying may bring them their special blanket, assuming that because the blanket makes them happy, it will also make the crying person happy. In this way the child is egocentric, but not selfish.

Social learning theory is the extension of the euphemism actions speak louder than words. If your mother drinks, even though she tells you it is bad and you should not do it, you are likely to become a drinker based on her example.

Modeling is observing someone's, our parents' or our peer's, behavior, and basing our own behavior on it. Bandura's also had a theory called Reciprocal Determinism which is the interaction of a person's personality, the environment and the behavior. An example of this theory is an outgoing person will interact with the environment, say a hotel desk clerk, differently than a shy person. The way they interact determines the outcome, possibly a room upgrade which reinforces their outgoing personality, i.e., if I'm funny and outgoing I get extra privileges. A shy person would not have the same reaction because they would not handle the situation the same way. A shy person would not even attempt to do what an outgoing person would do, hence the reaction is different.

Explicit role instruction (stereotypes): boys play with trucks and cars, girls wear makeup.

Lewis Terman conducted a longitudinal study of smart kids. The results are that the children are happy adults.

Baby Albert. There once was a boy who was kept in a box. By using classical conditioning, the researchers made the baby afraid of rats. Later because of stimulus generalization, he was afraid of all furry animals. Most children's fears are learned through conditioning. This is a good example of horrendous research ethics.

Stimulus Generalization is when something from conditioning carries over to another related area. You are afraid of spiders; soon you become afraid of all bugs.

Lev Vygotsky developed the theory of social development or social cognition. He stated that every function in the child's cultural development appears twice: first, between people and then inside the child. There were three elements to his theory. First, the idea that social interaction facilitates cognitive improvement. In other words, social learning, or the cultural aspect of a child's life which occurs outside their body, happens before development, which occurs inside the child. The second aspect is the presence of a "More Knowledgeable Other" (MKO). This person is more knowledgeable than the child is in a specific area. It could be a parent, teacher, coach, friend, or even a computer. The third element is the "Zone of Proximal Development" (ZPD). This describes the fact that there is a gap between what the child can do with help, and what they can do on their own. When the child closes the gap, they have learned.

Language Development

Language development begins at about six months. In all areas of the world and in the various cultures, babies start cooing and babbling at six months. This is called pre-speech. The first element of development is the cooing. The second development is babbling. The third is hollow phrases. The fourth is telegraphic speech. Children in early language development are not able to understand figurative language, but they do understand some grammar. One example is the children's book where the main character is told to do a household chore. She is told to "run over these sheets with the iron" and she does just that, holds the iron in her hand and tramples the sheets. To learn more about language development, turn to suffix 1 to read additional information about the stages.

Infants make various sounds, but around the age of six or seven months, these sounds begin including the repetition of meaningful sounds, such as "ma-ma" and "da-da." This stage of language development is described as babbling.

Along with the babbling comes gestures. During the period from 6 to 12 months old infants become increasingly proficient at making their wants clear through their gestures.

It is also interesting to note that children understand much of what is said to them, even before they are able to speak. For example, when asked "where's mommy?" a 10 month old will look in her direction. Most infants can also understand the word "no" long before they can talk.

Most children can speak a few, generally unclear, words by the age of one. By 18 months the vocabulary will expand to around 50 words. From here a child's vocabulary will begin to expand rapidly, reaching rates as high as 100 words a month. As infants are learning to speak, it is common for them to use holophrase speaking patterns combined with tone to get their meaning across. About six months after speaking their first words, children begin to string words together. All children learn at different rates, but the real indicator of proficiency is the ability to communicate, not the extent of vocabulary.

There are three main theories about language development. The first follows the idea of operant conditioning. Because babies are rewarded with attention or food when they say "mama" and "baba" they will continue to say those words and learn new ones. The other theory is that language abilities develop innately. This theory comes from Noam Chomsky, and states that since children all learn language rapidly, and around the same ages, there must be some mechanism in the brain which aids in language acquisition. Recent research has shown that language acquisition is likely just as much a result of either of these theories as it is of the social aspect of language. Children learn to speak from listening to their parents, especially through "baby talk," a term which describes not how infants sound, but how adults speak to infants. Infants learn early on to distinguish between the distinct sounds which are important to whichever language is spoken around them the most.

Echolalia is a baby repeating what you just said. At 10-14 months most children begin to speak actual words. Chomsky stated that the ability to develop language skills is inherited in genes. Language theorists believe that a child acquires language through reinforcement from their environment. This would include all people they come in contact with and other things like television.

The study of language is rather complex. The scientific study of words and sentences is called semantics. Opposites, synonyms, antonyms, and how sentences are put together are all subjects will fall under semantics. Holophrase syntax describes a communication style in which single words are used to communicate. This is typical of toddlers learning how to speak, for example "give" or "mama." The meaning is still understood, even though complete sentences are not used.

Morphemes are the smallest unit of a word which has meaning. Morphemes can be bound or free. A bound morpheme must be with a word. For example, in the word "impossible" the morpheme "im" is bound because it cannot be said alone. However, in the word "shipment" the morpheme ship is free because it can be a word on its own. Even smaller than morphemes, phonemes are also an area of study. Phonemes are the individual sounds. For example, in English there are 40 phonemes, created with different combinations of the 26 letters.

The repetition of certain syllables is called babbling. In hearing children, babbling begins around the age of six or seven months. However in deaf infants, babbling sounds don't occur until several months later. It is believed, however, that deaf infants do make the motions of babbling around the same time, even though they don't vocalize it. Deaf infants also become much more proficient at communicating through gestures than do hearing infants. When parents sign to deaf children, by the time they are ten months old, they often begin to demonstrate the basic signs of American Sign Language.

Child Learning

Children learn and form their conscience to represent values communicated by parents. Children watch their parents for cues for their actions and knowledge of what is acceptable behavior. Actions really do speak louder than words. The best way to teach children values is to do as one believes is correct.

Some children learn aggression through their peers. Think about that before you put your kids in daycare. Even children who learn to tolerate frustration can learn aggressive behavior.

Kibbutz

A Kibbutz is where a group of people live together and the children of all the people are raised by one or two people. The real parents of the children may see them for one hour a day. This is referred to as the hour of love. Think of modern day daycare. Children that are raised on the Kibbutz are used to study the effects of multiple caretakers. For example, they have more bland personality types because they have had to get along with their "new family." It is also difficult for them to create and maintain intimate relationships as they have a lack of emotional depth.

Childhood

New infants tend to monopolize their parent's time. Every time they need something, a parent is there to comply. As the infant grows into a toddler, the routine changes. Sometimes they have to wait for something they didn't have to before and sometimes they are even told no. This can be a confusing or frustrating time for children, and this is the origin of the temper tantrum. In young children, a tantrum is less an expression of defiance (as it may be when they grow older) than it is an expression of anger or frustration.

A **hurried child** is always in a hurry, eat, get ready, wash your face, etc. A **resilient child** is one that bounces back from a difficult situation like abuse. A **rite of passage** signals to society that certain rules have changed. This person is no longer a child. Examples can be getting a driver's license, first job, first date, getting married, etc.

Childhood depression can be expressed as "nobody likes me."

The most direct measure of syntax in middle childhood the mean link of the utterance. (how long their sentences are).

Psychometrics: cultural bias not generally known across all subcultures.

Mainstreaming: putting disabled students with normal students.

Children are most likely to achieve if their parents have set high standards and assist the children along the way. Gifted children often hide gifts to fit in.

Psychological maltreatment: not physical abuse but when the child feels rejected or feels failure.

Self-concept: Who am I? Self-aware, recognized, defined.

Self-esteem: begins in middle childhood.

Peer group: an environment where children live and attend school.

Stages of friendship:

0 Momentary playmates 3-7
One way assistance 4-9
Two way, fair weather 6-12
Intimate 9-15
Autonomous, interdependent 12+

The older a child becomes the more distinct their friendship circle grows. Preschool children will often claim to have many friends, and engage in generalizations such as everyone in their class being their friend. Then, by the time they are eight, children will have developed more defined circles of friends, and by the time they are ten will identify with specific "best" friends. This pattern is especially pronounced in girls, and by the time they have reached middle childhood, most girls will identify one and only one best friend.

Behavior of a child with a difficult temperament can be managed by patient and consistent parenting. The amount of positive and helpful behavior of school-aged children correlates with the child's history of socialization. If someone wants to develop a secure attachment to a child, they must respond appropriately to their signals like picking up a baby when it cries. A father's role with an infant usually involves more play. Firstborn children are more likely to be motivated to achieve. Sibling rivalry is related to the ages of the children. Most children grow out of it.

John Bowlby's attachment theory states that infants need to form at least one strong attachment, such as to a parent, in order to develop normally. He also believed that the attachment held evolutionary purpose. The infant tends to want proximity to the person who cares for them as a form of self-preservation. According to Bowlby's theory, if a child feels that their caregiver is nearby and attentive, they feel confident to explore their surroundings. If not, they feel anxious and over extended time periods, become depressed.

Most infants engage in a type of entertainment which has been termed **parallel play**. In parallel play, two (or more) children sit side by side, or near each other, and play without interacting with the other child or trying to influence them in any way. They may occasionally look at one another or see what each other are doing, but for the most part will stay in their own area and entertain themselves. This is the normal type of behavior until around the age of three when children begin to engage in associative play, where they share their toys and begin to interact more.

The controversy between putting a child in daycare versus keeping them at home with a parent raises many questions, with strong opinions for both sides. Every situation is different. In some cases, it is necessary for households to have two incomes, creating a need for daycare services, and in other cases daycare services cannot be afforded, meaning a parent must remain at home with the child. According to the 2000 census report, 48% of children younger than two were cared for solely by a parent. Many experts believe that there is no substitute for the constant presence of a mother in a young child's life. Studies have shown that children who remain at home are less aggressive and get sick less often than children who are in daycare. On the other hand, often children in daycare have larger vocabulary skills and are more socially developed than children who are not. Some argue that children in daycare have higher cognitive development as well. However, daycare can also decrease a child's relationship with their mother. In any case, the most important factor seems to be the quality of care which the child receives, more than the type of care.

Institutionalized children. The negative effects of sensory deprivation (not as much attention) are more likely to increase with the length of the stage. Failure to thrive is caused by emotional neglect. They can look healthy but not be thriving. Children are easily stressed concerning divorce, moving and death.

Some health problems that children can get (duration ranging from 1 to 14 days) are measles, whooping cough, mumps, polio, and diphtheria. School exposure can help spread epidemics and colds. Ninety-percent of all children in kindergarten are immunized.

Deferred imitation: imitation of a past-observed behavior. A child may see their mother breastfeeding a sibling and may later copy the action with a doll.

Read to children to teach them to read. The Montessori method was created when teachers worked with mentally retarded kids. The teachers gave five-year-olds an Italian national exam and had success. The Montessori method teaches children to realize their full abilities.

Your identity changes as you are socialized (grow up). Family therapy involves the whole family. Some children have emotional disturbances while growing up, including bed-wetting, tics and stuttering. **Gender identity:** the awareness of being a male or female. **Gender conservation:** child's realization their sex will stay the same.

There are different types of child play. They are in chronological order:

- Unoccupied behavior
- Onlooker
- Solitary independent (plays alone)
- Parallel play (plays around others but not with them)
- Associative
- Cooperative play

Fear of the dark. For children about six years old, the fear is strong and can appear suddenly. This is what you should do:

- Accept the fear as normal

- Offer reassurance

- Encourage emotions and their expression

PARENTING STYLES

Authoritarian: "because I say so" – more prevalent in lower-class families.

Permissive: makes few demands, hardly ever punishes.

Authoritative: respects individuality, but tries to instill social values.

Disease

Hypokinetic diseases are defined as diseases which are either related to or caused by a sedentary lifestyle. In other words, hypokinetic diseases are caused by the lack of regular exercise or activity. Some hypokinetic diseases are joint disorders, obesity, coronary heart disease, diabetes, and high blood pressure.

Divorce

When children are in the preoperational stage, ages 3-6, they are egocentric and will, therefore, think divorce is their fault. A male living with a single mom needs more affection. Girls living with single moms have difficulties with relationships with males in adolescence.

BENEFITS FOR EMPLOYED MOTHERS:

1. Mothers get confidence and satisfaction
2. Relieves financial pressure
3. Children are offered a wider variety of role models

Aging

Gerontology is the study of the aging process. Every moment we change, we age and grow a little older and hopefully, a little smarter. As our bodies change so do our lifestyle and our priorities. People who are working that experience discrimination because of their age, regardless if they are considered too old or too young, are victims of what is called ageism.

Gerontologists have determined three categories of old age:

- Young-old: 65-74
- Middle-old: 75-84
- Old-old: 85+

The elderly are a huge growing segment of the population. This creates many concerns regarding Medicare and Social Security. Will these programs be around for new generations or will they become bankrupt? Another factor that has occurred with the growth of this age group is the need for new businesses focused on the needs and wants of the aged. In-home health care has growth substantially as have other service areas.

Biological theories of aging:

- Wear-and-tear theory: like everything else in the world, the human body wears out.
- Cellular theory: we only have a certain number of cells, which are programmed to only replicate so many times before they are finished and the body begins to deteriorate.
- Autoimmune theory: as our bodies age, our immune systems become less effective at fighting disease, stress, etc.
- Genetic mutation: the number of cells that have problems or mutations that increase with age.

Osteoporosis is a disorder where the bones are weakened and become porous, like a sponge.

Alzheimer's disease is a chronic condition that deteriorates the nerve fibers in the brain controlling memory, speech, and personality. The early symptoms of Alzheimer's

disease include personality changes, lack of interest in activities, and change in sleep patterns, and are often confused with depression. Alzheimer's disease affects nearly half of all people over 85. People with this condition experience memory loss, disorientation and personality changes. Once the disease strikes, the victim's life expectancy is cut in half. Currently, there is little that can be done to treat this condition.

Strategies for healthy aging include:

- Developing and maintaining healthy relationships

- Enriching your spiritual life

- Improving physical fitness

As a person ages, many of the first and most visible signs of aging relate to the skin or appearance. As a person ages, skin becomes dryer, thinner, and less elastic, which causes aging. A second marker is "age spots," so named because they appear as dark patches of skin as a person ages. These changes in the skin are heightened with exposure to sun, and people who spend, or spent, a lot of time in the sun. Another dramatic change occurs in the hair, as it becomes thinner and grayer, for some eventually turning white.

Death and Bereavement

Many people fear death. In fact, this is the leading of many fears, including fear of public speaking, spiders, heights, confined spaces, etc. There are stages that a person goes through when they find out they have an incurable disease or find out they are going to die. These stages are also known as Kübler-Ross's Stages of Dying, which are:

1. Denial (shock) "This could never happen to me. This must be a mistake."

2. Anger (emotion) "This is unfair. Why me?"

3. Bargaining "If you don't die I will do the following…"

4. Preparatory Depression "There's nothing I can do about this."

5. Acceptance "I'm ready."

We each deal with death in "our own way" but go through the same stages which are very similar. Here are the stages:

1. Frozen feelings
2. Emotional release

3. Loneliness
4. Physical symptoms
5. Guilt
6. Panic
7. Hostility
8. Selective memory
9. Struggle for new life pattern
10. A feeling that life is good!

Hospice is where nursing care is given meant to maximize the quality of life for those who are dying.

When planning for death, certain issues of business must be attended to. A will, basically one's wishes for the distribution of one's property and possessions after death, should be written and entrusted to the family attorney. This will prevent you from dying intestate, or without a will. If wanted, a living will, a document that states your wishes about wanting to be put on life support or termination of such support, can be created. This also should be entrusted to family and to an attorney. It is important to discuss those wishes with your family so that there can be an understanding of your wishes. Organ donation or body donation are other possibilities that you may wish to consider. Discussing your wants for funeral arrangements will help prepare your family for when that day comes.

Kohlberg's Theory of Moral Development

Level 1: Preconventional morality

Stage 1: Punishment and obedience phase. Whether you will be punished or not determines what is moral or not. For example, you don't speed when driving the car because you know that you might get a ticket, a negative sanction from an authority figure.

Stage 2: A person becomes aware of two different viewpoints. You see the right action as what satisfies your personal needs. You don't speed while driving a car because you want the lower rates on car insurance that you will get having no tickets on your record.

Level 2: Conventional morality

Stage 3: A "good boy-good girl" orientation. You do what is right in order to gain status or approval from other people or society. For example, you don't get speeding tickets while driving because in your circle of friends that would make you appear irresponsible, therefore lowering your social status.

Stage 4: Social-order-maintaining orientation. A person abides by the law because they think that law is a higher order. It is their duty as a responsible citizen to not speed. This type of person would not run a red light in a deserted intersection even if he had been waiting five minutes. They believe that laws cannot be broken under any circumstance.

Level 3: Postconventional morality

Stage 5: The social contract orientation. A person is concerned with how their action might affect society. "I'm not going to speed because I might get into an accident and injure someone."

Stage 6: The universal ethical principle orientation. A person makes decisions according to his or her conscience. Not many, if any, people get to this stage.

Kohlberg believed that you go through these stages one at a time and can not skip them.[d] According to both Kohlberg and Piaget, the most immature reason to do something is to avoid punishment.

Morality of Care

One critique of Kohlberg's theory comes from Carol Gilligan. Gilligan disagreed with Kohlberg's theory because his subjects were mainly male. She believed that his theory was an apt description for the male progression, which she called the morality of justice. However, she believed that women followed a different system, which she called morality of care. Gilligan believed that women did progress through similar stages, however their conflict was between self and other, while for men the conflict was between self and justice.

Conducting Studies

Case Study

In a case study, a single individual (subject) is intensely studied. The researcher gets data through personal interviews with the subject, its employees, neighbors, contacts, etc., and by reviewing documentation or records (i.e., medical history, family life, etc.). Other sources for information are testing and direct observation of the subject. **Case studies used by Piaget and Freud led to wrong conclusions because they were not scientifically performed.**

Survey

A survey is a great way to get information about a specific type of information. For example, a survey would work well to measure performance in an office environment. These can be aggregated and used to improve employee performance. Usually with a survey, questionnaires are given out to participants who are then asked to answer questions to the best of their ability. When a participant fills out a survey themselves *about* themselves, it is called self-report data. This information can possibly not be as reliable as other research methods because subjects may be dishonest with their answers. For example, the question "Are you ever late to work?" may have respondents answering "no" when in fact, they are late but either do not remember that or are dishonest to avoid punishment or negative information about themselves. Many give the answers they feel that researchers (or themselves) want to hear instead of the truth.

Naturalistic Observation

Jean Piaget extensively used natural observation to study children. Naturalistic observation is when a researcher observes and studies subjects without interacting or interfering with them. Piaget observed the behavior of children playing in the schoolyard to assess developmental stages. Another example well known to television viewers of the series "Star Trek" involves "The Prime Directive." This is the most perfect version demonstrated (in fiction) of naturalistic observation. In the show, the researchers had the ability to view and study human cultures without being known to the subjects because of their advancements in technology. In the series, it was a great violation to interact with and impact the development of these cultures and societies.

Laboratory Observation

Laboratory observation is conducted in a laboratory environment. This method is selected to monitor specific biological changes in individuals. In a lab setting, expensive and sophisticated machinery can be used to study the participants. Sometimes one-way mirrors are used to observe the participants.

Psychological Tests

Psychological tests give information about participants. Some of the more common include standardized tests such as the Minnesota Multiphasic Personality Inventory also known as the MMPI (a personality test), aptitudes, interests, etc. A participant's score is then compared to the norms for that test. A test is valid if it measures what it is supposed to. For example, a test on depression will be able to measure a person's depression. If it cannot, then the test is not valid. Content validity is applied when a test measures something with more that one facet. For example, a test for overall cooking skills would not be valid if it only tested baking cakes and not other skills such as grilling meat or making soup.

Cross Sectional Studies

When people of different ages are studied at one particular time it is called a cross sectional study, because you have a cross section of the population or demographic that you want to study.

Longitudinal Studies

Longitudinal studies are when people are followed and studied over a long period of time and checked up on at certain points. These are best used to study the development of certain traits and track health issues. An example of a longitudinal study would be: 600 infants that were put up for adoption were tracked for several years. Some infants were adopted, some returned to the birth mothers and some were put into foster care. Which group adjusted the best and why? Lewis Terman did a longitudinal study of smart kids. The results are that the children are happy adults.

Correlation Research

Correlation research is used to show links between events, people, actions, behaviors, etc. Correlation research does not determine the causes of behavior but is linked to statistics. Causation is the cause of something. Correlation is not causation. This is an example of FAULTY, incorrect causation: a child eats an ice cream three times a week. This child scores well on school aptitude tests. It is determined that eating ice cream will make you smarter and do better on tests. There are additional factors or many others including socioeconomic status resulting from educated parents who genetically pass on their aptitude for school as well as their influence on the importance of school. In this situation, it is most likely the parents who contribute to the child's aptitude scores.

When conducting a survey and you have completed compiling the data, you will be able to measure the correlation between certain traits and variables tested. A correlation coefficient measures the strength between the two variables. A correlation coefficient is a number between -1 and +1.

A **positive correlation** means that when one variable increases, the other variable increases as well. For example, the more a couple fights, the more likely they are to get a divorce.

When one variable increases and the other variable decreases it is called a **negative correlation.** An example of this would be babies that are held by their caregivers tend to cry less. When the amount of time they are held goes up, the time they cry goes down.

The higher the number of the correlation coefficient, the stronger the correlation. A +0.9 or -0.9 shows a very strong correlation because the number is closest to a whole positive number 1 or a whole negative number 1. A weak correlation is a +0.1 or a -0.1. A correlation of zero shows that there is no relationship between variables.

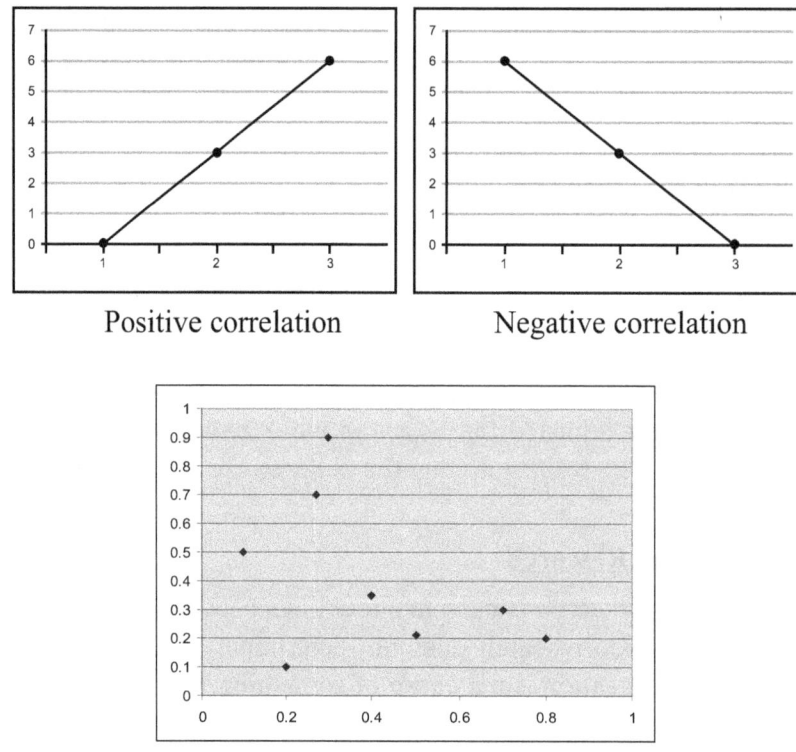

Positive correlation   Negative correlation

No correlation

Census

A census is a collection of data from all cases or people in the chosen set. Usually, the most common form of a census would take place within an entire school or state. This means that every person of that school or state must be included. Censuses are usually not performed because they are so expensive. A census is valuable because it gives an accurate representation. To save time and money, survey companies will ask 1000 people or so (remember, the number changes based on the amount of people to be surveyed. A good rule of thumb is 10%). This is called sampling. For example, a recent census shows that the single person is the fastest-growing household type. So basically, a sample is a set of cases of people randomly chosen from a large group. The sample is to represent the group. The larger the sample, the more accurate the results.

READING CHARTS AND GRAPHS

Charts and graphs are easy ways to display information and make it easily readable.

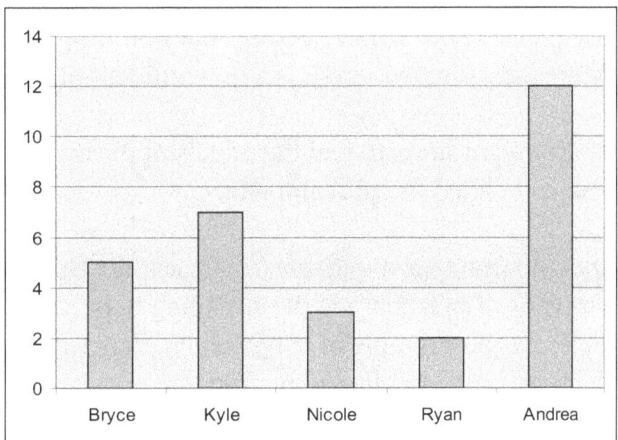

The above is a bar chart which shows five student's hours per week that they practice the piano. Are you able to tell who has the most hours and who has the least? How many hours per week does Nicole practice?

Name	Hours Per Week
Andrea	12
Bryce	5
Kyle	7
Nicole	3
Ryan	2

EXPERIMENTS

In experiments, a researcher manipulates variables to test theories and conclusions. Each experiment has independent and dependent variables. This is how researchers test cause and effect links and relationships.

The independent variable is the variable that researchers have direct control over. The dependent variable is then observed by the researcher.

In experiments, there are usually two groups of participants. One group is the experimental group and one group is the control group. The most common example is in medical trials. Let's say there is a trial run of a new diet drug. The researcher will split the group randomly in two. Group 1 will receive the diet pill that is being tested. Group 2 will receive a placebo pill. The placebo pill is simply a sugar pill. Group 2 will not know that they are not receiving the real drug. This allows the researchers to study the true effectiveness and side-effects of the pill. When the people are assigned to a group randomly, it is called **random assignment**. This particular experiment was a single-blind experiment. A **double-blind** experiment is when none of the doctors, researches and participants know who is getting the real drug. It is assigned by computer or an independent individual where it is kept confidential until the conclusion of the study.

When a participant starts to feel the effects of the drug but is *actually* taking a sugar pill or placebo it is called the **placebo effect**.

It is very important to avoid bias in research. Bias is the distortion of the results. Common types of bias include the sampling bias, subject bias and researcher bias. The placebo effect is an example of subject bias. Experimenter or researcher bias is avoided by conducting a double-blind experiment.

There are some disadvantages to experiments. They cannot be used to study everything. There are officially defined rules how humans and animals must be treated with the experiment. In an infamous experiment by psychologist Stanley Milgram, subjects were told that they were giving painful electric shocks to other people when in reality they were not. Some people consider this experiment unethical because it caused the participants emotional discomfort.

Researchers must get consent from their participants before conducting experiment. Informed consent means that the participants must know the content of the experiment and be warned of any risk or harm.

The **independent variable** in a study is the researchers have direct control over.

Dependent variables are all other variables. The higher the correlation between the two factors is, the more closely the movement of one effects the movement of others.

Quantitative is a term used in research. It is used to describe something measurable, usually expressed as a number.

Qualitative is a term used to describe something similar in structure or organization.

SCIENTIFIC METHOD IS COMPRISED OF FOUR STEPS:

1. Gather information
2. Generate hypothesis
3. Test hypothesis
4. Revise

Mean, median and mode are three important terms in analyzing and understanding data. The mean of a set of data is also called the average, because it is one method of determining the average or normal value for a set of data. To find an average, add all of the numbers in a data set and divide the total by the total number of data. For example the average of 3, 4, 5, and 6 is 3+4+5+6 which equals 28 divided by 4 because there are four numbers. 28/4= 4.5. Therefore, the average is 4.5.

The median is the middle number in a set of data. For example the median of the data set 3, 3, 4, 5, 6, 7, 8 is 5. The mode is the number which occurs the most often. For example, the mode of the data set 3, 3, 4, 5, 6, 6, 6, 7, 8, 9, 9 is 6 because it is the only number which occurs three times. All three are used together to give an accurate representation of the data.

Sample Test Questions

1) Which person believed that children were born a blank slate?

   A) Jean-Jacques Rousseau
   B) John Locke
   C) Alfred Binet
   D) Sigmund Freud

The correct answer is B:) John Locke.

2) At what age will most children begin to identify which a/some specific best friend(s)?

   A) 4 years old
   B) 6 years old
   C) 8 years old
   D) 10 years old

The correct answer is D:) 10 years old. For girls especially, by the time they are ten, they will identify only one "best" friend.

3) Which of the following correctly orders Kohlberg's three levels of moral development?

   A) Preconventional, conventional, postconventional
   B) Preconventional, postconventional, conventional
   C) Conventional, preconventional, postconventional
   D) Conventional, postconventional, preconventional

The correct answer is A:) Preconventional, conventional, postconventional.

4) Trust vs. Mistrust is Erikson's developmental stage which occurs while a

   A) Infant
   B) Toddler
   C) Preschooler
   D) School-age child

The correct answer is A:) Infant.

5) Which of the following correctly lists Piaget's four stages of cognitive development?

   A) Sensorimotor, preoperational, formal operational, concrete operational
   B) Concrete operational, sensorimotor, preoperational, formal operational
   C) Preoperational, sensorimotor, concrete operational, formal operational
   C) Sensorimotor, preoperational, concrete operational, formal operational

The correct answer is D:) Sensorimotor, preoperational, concrete operational, formal operational.

6) _____ is the earliest sound a child makes to communicate?

   A) Babbling
   B) Cooing
   C) Echolalia
   D) Crying

The correct answer is D:) Crying.

7) Which of the following is NOT an example of cross-modal perception?

   A) A child feels an object, and when they later see it, they recognize it.
   B) A child plays with an object and later chooses to play with it again.
   C) A child chews on an object and later identifies how it feels.
   C) A child hears a person and looks around the room to find them.

The correct answer is B:) A child plays with an object and later chooses to play with it again. This answer involves the same area of knowledge, whereas answers A, C, and D involve two areas.

8) _____ is the ethical component of personality and provides moral standards.

   A) Id
   B) Ego
   C) Superego
   D) Id and ego

The correct answer is C:) Superego.

9) At approximately what age do children begin communicating through telegraphic speech?

    6 months
    1 year
    2 years
    D) 4 years

The correct answer is C:) 2 years. Telegraphic speech contains simple two word sentences. While children may have a large vocabulary, their sentences remain simple as their understanding of language continues to develop.

10) The belief that you are the center of the universe

    A) Assimilation
    B) Accommodation
    C) Classification
    D) Egocentrism

The correct answer is D:) Egocentrism.

11) At what stage of pregnancy are syphilis and rubella the most dangerous?

    A) First trimester
    B) Second trimester
    C) Early third trimester
    D) End third trimester

The correct answer is A:) First trimester.

12) Relating new information to something familiar is called

    A) Assimilation
    B) Accommodation
    C) Learning
    D) Elaboration

The correct answer is D:) Elaboration.

13) Organized, logical thought is a part of which of Piaget's stages of development?

   A) Sensory motor
   B) Preoperational
   C) Concrete operational
   D) Formal operational

The correct answer is C:) Concrete operational.

14) A statistical measure of typical scores for categories of information

   A) Class inclusion
   B) Conservation
   C) Developmental norm
   D) Egocentrism

The correct answer is C:) Developmental norm.

15) Which of the following correctly describes humanism?

   A) A theory that revolves around the individual's unconscious motivation.
   B) The belief that all people are inherently good and are motivated to achieve their full potential.
   C) The study of observable behavior.
   D) Examines how the mind knows, thinks, learns, remembers, and relates to behavior.

The correct answer is B:) The belief that all people are inherently good and are motivated to achieve their full potential.

16) Temperament in infants is measured by monitoring

   A) Activity level
   B) Irritability
   C) Social responsiveness
   D) All of the above

The correct answer is D:) All of the above.

17) Who developed the idea of fluid and crystallized intelligence?

   A) Raymond Cattell
   B) John Bowlby
   C) Lev Vygotsky
   D) Jean Piaget

The correct answer is A:) Raymond Cattell. Bowlby developed the attachment theory, Vygotsky developed a theory of social development, Piaget developed a theory of cognitive development, and Maslow developed the hierarchy of needs.

18) The first three weeks of prenatal growth are known as?

   A) Growing period
   B) Germinal period
   C) Fetus period
   D) Neonate period

The correct answer is B:) Germinal period.

19) Which of the following personality traits is NOT typical of divergent thinking?

   A) Persistent
   B) Curious
   C) Structured
   D) Nonconformist

The correct answer is C:) Structured. Answers A, B and D all describes personality traits associated with divergent thinking.

20) The process of being able to identify something encountered before

   A) Operation
   B) Recognition
   C) Recall
   D) Schema

The correct answer is B:) Recognition.

21) Generativity vs. Stagnation is Erikson's developmental stage which occurs while a

   A) School-age child
   B) Adolescent
   C) Young adult
   D) Middle-age adult

The correct answer is D:) Middle-age adult.

22) A set of perceptions, ideas or actions which go together

   A) Operation
   B) Recognition
   C) Recall
   D) Schema

The correct answer is D:) Schema.

23) A child who perceives the world only from their own point of view is

   A) Selfish
   B) Egocentric
   C) Dialectical
   D) Divergent

The correct answer is B:) Egocentric. Egocentric does not necessarily mean selfish.

24) Which of the following statements is the best example of telegraphic speech?

   A) My oldest and prettiest sister will visit with us next week
   B) My sister will visit next week
   C) Sister visit week
   D) My sister will be coming to visit me next week for three days

The correct answer is C:) Sister visit week. Telegraphic speech is a speech pattern which eliminates function words, and keeps only the content words of a sentence.

25) In which of the following situations would convergent thinking NOT be the most useful?

   A) Determining the correct answer on a physics test.
   B) Producing an abstract piece of artwork in painting class.
   C) Performing algebraic expressions in a math class.
   D) Taking a multiple choice test in a given amount of time.

The correct answer is B:) Producing an abstract piece of artwork in painting class. Art requires creativity, whereas in all of the other options, logical process would be more useful than creativity.

26) According to Freud, at what age does the oral stage occur?

   A) Birth to 1 year old
   B) 1-3 years old
   C) 3-6 years old
   D) 6-11 years old

The correct answer is A:) Birth to 1 year old.

27) Which of the following BEST describes the concrete operational stage of cognitive development?

   A) The world is understood in terms of physical existence and manipulation.
   B) Imagination and symbolic thinking increase understanding of concepts.
   C) Rationality and logical operations and principles are applied to the world.
   D) Abstract and hypothetical situations help in understanding many points of view.

The correct answer is C:) Rationality and logical operations and principles are applied to the world. Answer A describes the sensorimotor stage, answer B describes the preoperational stage, and answer D describes the formal operational stage.

28) Which is the second stage of Maslow's Hierarchy of Needs?

   A) Self-actualization
   B) Esteem needs
   C) Belonging and love
   D) Safety

The correct answer is D:) Safety.

29) What are the elements of dialectical perspective?

   A) Thesis and antithesis
   B) Preconventional thesis and post conventional thesis
   C) Androgyny, thesis and synthesis
   D) Thesis, antithesis and synthesis

The correct answer is D:) Thesis, antithesis, and synthesis. Dialectical perspective acknowledges two sides to an issue and creates an opinion by synthesizing them.

30) Which defense mechanism occurs when someone hides their feelings and does not acknowledge them?

   A) Denial
   B) Suppression
   C) Reaction formation
   D) Projection

The correct answer is B:) Suppression.

31) A parent notices that their children never do their homework, and instead spend all of their time playing on the computer. How could they apply the Premack principle?

   A) By allowing their children to do their homework after they have gotten bored with the computer.
   B) By grounding their children from the computer so that they are then forced to do their homework.
   C) By accepting that their children do not enjoy homework and allowing them to play quite often.
   D) By not allowing their children to play on the computer until their homework has been completed.

The correct answer is D:) By not allowing their children to play on the computer until their homework has been completed. The Premack principle uses a desired activity, such as the computer, as a reinforcer to make a less desired activity, such as homework, more probable.

32) Which of the following BEST describes parallel play?

   A) Children sit playing side by side completely unaware and unconcerned with one another.
   B) Children wish to exert complete control over one another's play and become aggressive.
   C) Children share their toys and interact with each other, but do not try to exert control.
   D) Children play side by side and are aware of each other, but do not wish to influence each other's play.

The correct answer is D:) Children play side by side and are aware of each other, but do not wish to influence each other's play.

33) What type of research is conducted by watching the subject?

   A) Naturalistic observation
   B) Longitudinal research
   C) Conditioning
   D) Operant conditioning

The correct answer is A:) Naturalistic observation.

34) Which of the following beliefs was developed by Carol Gilligan?

   A) Morality of Justice
   B) Morality of Law
   C) Morality of Care
   D) Morality of Opinion

The correct answer is C:) Morality of Care. Gilligan developed this system to describe the moral development and understand of women. She named Kohlberg's system the Morality of Justice.

35) Which defense mechanism occurs when someone turns a feeling into the exact opposite feeling?

   A) Denial
   B) Suppression
   C) Reaction formation
   D) Projection

The correct answer is C:) Reaction formation.

36) Which of the following is NOT an effect of syphilis or rubella on the fetus?

   A) Miscarriage
   B) Kidney problems
   C) Stillbirths
   D) Deafness

The correct answer is B:) Kidney problems. A, C, D and E all list problems caused by syphilis and/or rubella.

37) In this type of study, a single individual (subject) is intensely studied.

   A) Case study
   B) Naturalistic observation
   C) Psychological test
   D) Longitudinal study

The correct answer is A:) Case study.

38) When a participant starts to feel the effects of a drug but is actually taking a sugar pill or it is called

   A) Placebo effect
   B) Habituation
   C) Wishful thinking syndrome
   D) Double-blind

The correct answer is A:) Placebo effect.

39) Which of the following best describes convergent thinking?

   A) Methodical
   B) Logical
   C) Organized
   D) All of the above

The correct answer is D:) All of the above. Convergent thinking follows a process to determine a correct answer.

40) Identity vs. Role Confusion is Erikson's developmental stage which occurs while during which age?

   A) Infant
   B) Toddler
   C) Preschooler
   D) Adolescent

The correct answer is D:) Adolescent.

41) Who was the father of genetics and inheritance?

   A) Gregor Mendel
   B) Wilhelm Wundt
   C) William James
   D) John Watson

The correct answer is A:) Gregor Mendel.

42) Which defense mechanism is characterized by turning a feeling into the exact opposite feeling?

   A) Projection
   B) Displacement
   C) Reaction formation
   D) Suppression

The correct answer is C:) Reaction formation.

43) Dyslexia is caused by a deficiency in understanding what component of language?

   A) Phonological
   B) Semantic
   C) Pragmatic
   D) Grammatical

The correct answer is A:) Phonological. This means that they have difficulty associating the appearance of a letter with the sound it makes.

44) Which defense mechanism occurs when someone redirects stress into a socially productive activity?

   A) Rationalization
   B) Regression
   C) Sublimation
   D) Projection

The correct answer is C:) Sublimation.

45) Initiative vs. Guilt is Erikson's developmental stage which occurs while a

   A) Infant
   B) Toddler
   C) Preschooler
   D) School-age child

The correct answer is C:) Preschooler.

46) What does ADHD stand for?

   A) Attention Deficiency Hyperactivity Disability
   B) Attention Disorder Hyperactivity Deficit
   C) Attention Deficit Hyperactivity Disorder
   D) Attention Deficiency Hyperactivity Disorder

The correct answer is C:) Attention Deficit Hyperactivity Disorder.

47) Which is the fourth stage of Maslow's Hierarchy of Needs?

   A) Self-actualization
   B) Esteem needs
   C) Belonging and love
   D) Safety

The correct answer is B:) Esteem needs.

48) Which of the following is most directly harmed by teratogens?

   A) Zygote
   B) Embryo
   C) Fetus
   D) Zygote and Embryo equally

The correct answer is C:) Fetus. Teratogens are harmful agents which can cause birth defects and are harmful to the fetus.

49) To help the eye focus, the lens changes its curves in a process called

   A) Absolute threshold
   B) Retinal adaptation
   C) Accommodation
   D) Habituation

The correct answer is C:) Accommodation.

50) In Erikson's theory, at what age would one struggle with initiative vs. guilt?

   A) Toddler
   B) Preschool
   C) School-age
   D) Young Adult

The correct answer is B:) Preschool.

51) Which of the following is an example of Maslow's first level of needs?

   A) Food
   B) School
   C) Car
   D) Travel

The correct answer is A:) Food.

52) Which of the following statements is NOT true?

   A) The original opinion about an idea or belief is called a thesis.
   B) An antithesis is the counter to the opinion in the thesis.
   C) Dialectical perspective allows for opinion change as new information is gathered.
   D) Dialectical perspective discourages firm opinions.

The correct answer is D:) Dialectical perspective discourages firm opinions. Although dialectical perspective acknowledges that opinions will change as information is gathered, it also supports the idea of still having a stated belief or opinion.

53) The ability to group objects together on the basis of common features

   A) Assimilation
   B) Accommodation
   C) Classification
   D) Conservation

The correct answer is C:) Classification.

54) When a young child feels frustrated or angry they will most likely

   A) Figure out their problems themselves when given time.
   B) Discuss their feelings calmly and rationally.
   C) Throw a temper tantrum.
   D) Wait patiently for help from a parent.

The correct answer is C:) Throw a temper tantrum. Tantrums are the most common way for young children to express their anger.

55) Endocrine glands create and release _____ into the bloodstream.

   A) Hormones
   B) Epinephrine
   C) Adrenaline
   D) Chemicals

The correct answer is D:) Chemicals.

56) The brain is a part of what system?

   A) Endocrine system
   B) Central nervous system
   C) Autonomic nervous system
   D) None of the above

The correct answer is B:) Central nervous system.

57) According to Freud, at what age does the phallic stage occur?

   A) Birth to 1 year old
   B) 1-3 years old
   C) 3-6 years old
   D) D) 6-11 years old

The correct answer is C:) 3-6 years old.

58) Which of the following is NOT a sign of aging?

   A) Wrinkles
   B) Less elastic skin
   C) Hardening of the fontanels
   D) Age spots

The correct answer is C:) Hardening of the fontanels. Fontanels are soft spots in a baby's skull.

59) Fear of the dark is strong for children of about what age?

   A) Newborns
   B) 2
   C) 4
   D) 6

The correct answer is D:) 6.

60) Which style of parent respects individuality, but tries to instill social values?

   A) Authoritarian
   B) Permissive
   C) Authoritative
   D) Detached

The correct answer is C:) Authoritative.

61) Which of the following is NOT true of reinforces?

   A) They can be positive or negative.
   B) They can be used as a method of learning.
   C) They make a behavior ore likely to occur.
   D) It must be tangible.

The correct answer is D:) It must be tangible.

62) Albert Bandura's famous study of Baby Albert demonstrated what?

   A) Social learning
   B) Classical conditioning
   C) Operant conditioning
   D) D) Object permanence

The correct answer is B:) Classical conditioning.

63) Which of the following is an example of Maslow's third level of needs?

   A) Sex
   B) Money
   C) Love
   D) Transportation

The correct answer is C:) Love.

64) Which of the following statements is FALSE?

   A) In some cases, it is necessary for households to have two incomes, creating a need for daycare services, while in other cases daycare services are too expensive.
   B) Children in daycare have larger vocabulary skills than children who are not.
   C) Studies have shown that children who remain at home are less aggressive than children in daycare.
   D) All of the above

The correct answer is D:) All of the above.

65) _____ is when a variable from conditioning carries over to another related area.

   A) Stimulus generalization
   B) Longitudinal research
   C) Conditioning
   D) Operant conditioning

The correct answer is A:) Stimulus generalization.

66) At approximately what age do children begin to babble?

   A) Two months old
   B) Four months old
   C) Six months old
   D) Twelve months old

The correct answer is C:) Six months old. At this age, the repetition of syllables such as "ma-ma-ma" is expected to begin.

67) Ritalin is a well-known drug used to treat

   A) Habituation
   B) Object permanence
   C) Hyperactivity
   D) Divergence

The correct answer is C:) Hyperactivity.

68) According to John Bowlby's attachment theory, if a child feels their caregiver is nearby and attentive

   A) They feel confident to explore their surroundings.
   B) It will not affect their behavior in any way.
   C) They feel stifled and will become depressed.
   D) They will fail to develop normally because they will always feel pressured.

The correct answer is A:) They feel confident to explore their surroundings. The attachment theory states that infants need to form at least one meaningful attachment to develop normally and feel confident.

69) When a baby repeats things that it has heard it is called

   A) Baby talk
   B) Echolalia
   C) Phonetic speech
   D) Speech pattern

The correct answer is B:) Echolalia.

70) Which of the following best describes divergent thinking?

   A) Creative
   B) Logical
   C) Organized
   D) Ambiguous

The correct answer is A:) Creative. Divergent thinking is a process where many ideas are brainstormed.

71) John Bowlby's attachment theory states that infants need to form strong attachment(s) in order to develop normally.

   A) One
   B) Two
   C) More than two
   D) None

The correct answer is A:) One.

72) Personality changes, lack of interest in activities, and change in sleep patterns are the early symptoms of

   A) Rubella
   B) Alzheimer's
   C) TSS
   D) Hypokinetic disease

The correct answer is B:) Alzheimer's.

73) By what age will both fontanels have hardened into bone?

   A) Two months old
   B) Eight months old
   C) Twelve months old
   D) Two years old

The correct answer is D:) Two years old. The posterior fontanel hardens within two months, but the anterior does not typically harden until age two.

74) Which of the following is NOT an example of fluid intelligence?

   A) Numerical problems
   B) Intellectual puzzles
   C) Creative responses
   D) Trivia knowledge

The correct answer is D:) Trivia knowledge. Factual information, such as trivia, is crystallized intelligence.

75) When something is measurable in number it is

   A) Naturalistic observation
   B) Qualitative
   C) Cross sectional studies
   D) Quantitative

The correct answer is D:) Quantitative.

76) Which of the following chromosome patterns would a person with Klinefelter's syndrome have?

A) XXY
B) XYY
C) XXX
D) XY

The correct answer is A:) XXY. This occurs with about 3 in every 1,000 males.

77) Which of the following represents that strongest correlation?

A) -.10
B) +.23
C) -.44
D) +.89

The correct answer is D:) +.89.

78) The Premack principle always relies on which of the following?

A) Androgyny
B) Positive punishment
C) Operant conditioning
D) Intrinsic reinforcers

The correct answer is C:) Operant conditioning. Intrinsic reinforcers are a part of operant conditioning, but the Premack principle can use extrinsic reinforcers as well, so C is the best answer.

79) Which is NOT a step in the scientific method?

A) Gather information
B) Generate hypothesis
C) Test hypothesis
D) None of the above

The correct answer is D:) None of the above.

80) Which of the following terms describes growth from the spine outward?

A) Acuital
B) Cephalocaudal
C) Proximodistal
D) Presbycusal

The correct answer is C:) Proximodistal. This means that the vital organs begin developing before the extremities do.

81) Which defense mechanism occurs when someone redirects their feelings, positive or negative, towards someone else?

A) Denial
B) Suppression
C) Reaction formation
D) Displacement

The correct answer is D:) Displacement.

82) According to Vygotsky's theory of social development, when does learning occur?

A) When a child sees the cultural aspect in society
B) When a child internalizes the cultural aspect
C) Through observing the more knowledgeable other
D) In the zone of proximal development

The correct answer is D:) In the zone of proximal development. The zone of proximal development (ZPD) describes the fact that there is a gap between what the child can do with help, and what they can do on their own. When the child closes the gap, they have learned.

83) From the bottom up, what are the stages of Maslow's hierarchy of needs?

A) Physical needs, esteem, belongingness and love, safety, self actualization
B) Physical needs, safety, esteem, belongingness and love, self actualization
C) Physical needs, safety, belongingness and love, esteem, self actualization
D) Physical needs, esteem, safety, belongingness and love, self actualization

The correct answer is C:) Physical needs, safety, belongingness and love, esteem, self actualization.

84) Classical conditioning describes a link between

   A) A stimulus and a response.
   B) An action and a consequence.
   C) An action and a reflexive response.
   D) A reflexive action and a consequence.

The correct answer is A:) A stimulus and a response.

85) Dr. Smith studied a brother and sister for three years. This represents

   A) Longitudinal research
   B) Cross sectional studies
   C) Naturalistic observation
   D) A case study

The correct answer is D:) A case study.

86) Language development begins at

   A) Birth
   B) Three months
   C) Six months
   D) One year

The correct answer is C:) Six months.

87) Children that are raised on the Kibbutz are used to study the effects of

   A) Imprinting
   B) Aggression in early childhood
   C) Attachment
   D) Multiple caretakers

The correct answer is D:) Multiple caretakers.

88) The process by which a person takes material into their mind from the environment is

   A) Assimilation
   B) Accommodation
   C) Classification
   D) Conservation

The correct answer is A:) Assimilation.

89) Which of the following is NOT a cause of ADHD?

   A) Lead poisoning
   B) Genetics
   C) Vitamin deficiency
   D) Creative personality

The correct answer is D:) Creative personality. Lead poisoning, genetics, vitamin deficiency and stressful environment are all causes of ADHD.

90) Which of the following best describes the attachment theory?

   A) Attachment to a parent is essential to development in infants.
   B) An infant's desire for proximity to the person who cares for them is a form of self-preservation.
   C) If an infant is separated from their main caregiver for an extended time, they will become depressed.
   D) All of the above.

The correct answer is D:) All of the above.

91) Which of the following relates to study of semantics?

   A) Synonyms
   B) Morphemes
   C) Antonyms
   D) All of the above

The correct answer is D:) All of the above. Semantics is the study of how words and sentences are put together and the more technical aspects of language. All of the answers are involved in semantics.

92) Men and women with androgynous personalities will

    A) Have very similar personality characteristics.
    B) Have traditional gender personality characteristics.
    C) Have personality characteristics opposite those traditional to their gender.
    D) Not follow any specific personality patterns.

The correct answer is A:) Have very similar personality characteristics.

93) What is the term for areas in a baby's skull where cartilage has not hardened into bone?

    A) Fontanels
    B) Karyotypes
    C) Myelin
    D) Miasmas

The correct answer is A:) Fontanels. This allows the plates of bone in the skull to flex during childbirth.

94) Which of the following best describes the intelligence level of a dyslexic person?

    A) Almost always below average
    B) Generally average or below average
    C) Average or above average
    D) Almost always above average

The correct answer is C:) Average or above average. People with dyslexia have average or above average intelligence, however their learning ability is impeded because of the disorder.

95) Which system is vulnerable for the most time after conception?

    A) Reproductive system
    B) Central nervous system
    C) Glandular system
    D) Digestive system

The correct answer is B:) Central nervous system.

96) Which of the following is a teratogen?

   A) Alcohol
   B) Tobacco
   C) HIV
   D) All of the above

The correct answer is D:) All of the above. Exposure to teratogens can cause many different and rather unpredictable side effects in unborn children.

97) In which stage of Kohlberg's theory of moral development is one concerned with avoiding punishment?

   A) Preoperational
   B) Preconventional
   C) Postconventional
   C) Conventional

The correct answer is B:) Preconventional.

98) Children in which stage of development will believe that the divorce of a parent is their fault due to egocentrism?

   A) Sensory motor
   B) Preoperational
   C) Concrete operational
   D) Formal operations

The correct answer is A:) Sensory motor.

99) Which of the following describes growth from the head downward?

   Acuital
   Cephalocaudal
   Proximodistal
   Presbycusis

The correct answer is B:) Cephalocaudal. This basically means that the head develops faster than the rest of the body.

100) An infant will look at an object that he prefers for than an object he has no interest in.

   A) A longer time
   B) A shorter time
   C) The same amount of time
   D) 30 seconds shorter

The correct answer is A:) A longer time.

101) What is cross-modal perception?

   A) Young children are likely to perceive the world from a self-centered perspective.
   B) An infant's desire for proximity to the person who cares for them is a form of self-preservation.
   C) Determining or imagining aspects of an object based on information from one area of knowledge.
   D) A specific type of dialectical thought which involves synthesizing two facts from different sources.

The correct answer is C:) Determining or imagining aspects of an object based on information from one area of knowledge.

102) According to Freud, at what age does the genital stage occur?

   A) Birth to 1 year old
   B) 1-3 years old
   C) 3-6 years old
   D) Adolescence

The correct answer is D:) Adolescence.

103) The early symptoms of Alzheimer's disease are often confused with which disorder?

   A) Depression
   B) Bipolar
   C) Heart failure
   D) Down syndrome

The correct answer is A:) Depression. They share symptoms such as personality changes, lack of interest in previously enjoyed activities, and forgetfulness.

104) Which of the following best describes hypokinetic diseases?

   A) A condition in which the brain begins to deteriorate in certain areas.
   B) Diseases which are either related to or caused by a sedentary lifestyle.
   C) Hypokinetic disease is a fancy term for the side effects of allergies.
   D) A spectrum of effects that can occur when a woman drinks during pregnancy.

The correct answer is B:) Diseases which are either related to or caused by a sedentary lifestyle. Answer A describes Alzheimer's disease, answer D describes FAS, and answer E describes Cholera.

105) When an infant no longer responds to a new toy he is showing

   A) Habituation
   B) Object permanence
   C) Hyperactivity
   D) Divergence

The correct answer is A:) Habituation.

106) Which of the following is NOT an element of Vygotsky's theory of social development?

   A) A child must see the cultural aspect in society
   B) A child must discuss the cultural aspect
   C) The MKO
   D) The ZPD

The correct answer is B:) A child must discuss the cultural aspect. Vygotsky's theory describes that the function occurs first outside, and then inside the child, but does not dictate that the child must discuss the aspect. The MKO and ZPD are elements of his theory however.

107) Which of the following statements is NOT correct?

   A) Even though deaf children do not vocally babble at the same age as hearing children, they do make the motions of babbling around the same age.
   B) Deaf infants tend to babble much more quietly than hearing children do.
   C) When parents begin communicating with infants through sign language, they begin to pick up on some of the most basic signs as early as ten months old.
   D) Deaf infants are much more proficient at communicating through gestures than hearing infants are.

The correct answer is B:) Deaf infants tend to babble much more quietly than hearing children do. Answers A, B and D give researched and proven facts, whereas answer B does not.

108) An infant startling at a noise is what type of reflex?

   A) Simple
   B) Beginning
   C) First level
   D) Second level

The correct answer is A:) Simple.

109) Which of the following is NOT characteristic of FAS?

   A) Poor coordination
   B) Learning disabilities
   C) Hyperactive behavior
   D) Liver failure

The correct answer is D:) Liver failure. Poor coordination, learning disabilities, hyperactive behavior, and having a large head are all possible FAS characteristics.

110) _____ theories are based on the idea that our actions are deeply influenced by our unconscious.

   A) Humanistic
   B) Psychoanalytical
   C) Cognitive
   D) Learning

The correct answer is B:) Psychoanalytical.

111) Which of the following is NOT an example of egocentrism?

   A) A child becomes upset when the sun "goes to bed early."
   B) A child cries when they drop a toy because they think they have hurt it.
   C) A child shares their teddy bear with a sad person because it always makes them happy.
   D) All of the above are examples of egocentrism.

The correct answer is D:) All of the above are examples of egocentrism. In each case the child understands the situation only from their own point of view.

112) Which of the following is NOT a factor of psychosocial health?

   A) Physical
   B) Spiritual
   C) Mental
   D) Emotional

The correct answer is A:) Physical.

113) What does FAS stand for?

   A) Fetal alcohol sickness
   B) Fetal addiction syndrome
   C) Fetal alcohol syndrome
   D) Fetal addiction sickness

The correct answer is C:) Fetal alcohol syndrome.

114) _____ theorists are concerned with the effects of various types of conditioning.

   A) Humanistic
   B) Psychoanalytical
   C) C) Cognitive
   D) D) Learning

The correct answer is D:) Learning.

115) Which of the following will cause the appearance of aging in the skin to be accelerated?

   A) Exposure to sun
   B) Lack of essential vitamins
   C) Medicine intake
   D) Increased water intake

The correct answer is A:) Exposure to sun. Age spots and dryness are particularly noticeable in people who spend or spent a lot of time in the sun.

116) Which of the following is a humanist?

   A) Maslow
   B) Freud
   C) Piaget
   D) Rogers

The correct answer is A:) Maslow.

117) Which of the following best describes the morphemes in the word unbreakable?

   A) 1 bound morpheme and 2 free morphemes
   B) 2 bound morphemes and 1 free morpheme
   C) 3 bound morphemes and no free morphemes
   D) No bound morphemes and 3 free morphemes

The correct answer is A:) 1 bound morphemes and 2 free morphemes. The morphemes are "un," "break" and "able." "Un" is bound, and "break" and "able" are free.

118) From week eight until conception is known as?

   A) Growing period
   B) Germinal period
   C) Fetus period
   D) Neonate period

The correct answer is C:) Fetus period.

119) Which of the following statements is FALSE?

   A) The older a child becomes, the more specific and distinct the friendship circle grows.
   B) When children are 10 years old they will generally begin to define one person as their best friend.
   C) Young children often have generalized definitions of friends, such as "all the people in my class."
   D) Boys are much more likely than girls to form close friendships with other people.

The correct answer is D:) Boys are much more likely than girls to form close friendships with other people. The truth is the exact opposite, girls are more likely to form close friendships.

120) Erik Erikson developed a theory involving how many stages of development?

   A) Four
   B) Five
   C) Eight
   D) Nine

The correct answer is C:) Eight.

121) The insulating sheath which helps transmit neural impulses is called

   A) Dendrite
   B) Neural coating
   C) Presbycusis
   D) Myelin

The correct answer is D:) Myelin. Myelin coats the neurons and dendrites.

122) What was the visual cliff experiment designed to test?

   A) An infant's depth perception
   B) An infant's auditory capabilities
   C) An infant's visual acuity
   D) An infant's mental capabilities

The correct answer is A:) An infant's depth perception.

123) According to Freud's personality theory, which of the following is present at birth?

A) Id
B) Ego
C) Superego
D) Id and ego

The correct answer is A:) Id.

124) Approximately what percent of children under two are cared for solely by a parent?

A) 10%
B) 20%
C) 38%
D) 48%

The correct answer is D:) 48%.

125) Which of the following is NOT considered a hypokinetic disease?

A) Obesity
B) Coronary heart disease
C) Cholera
D) Joint disorder

The correct answer is C:) Cholera. Cholera is an intestinal disease which is spread due to poor hygiene.

126) Social smile appears at how many weeks?

A) 2
B) 4
C) 7
D) 9

The correct answer is C:) 7.

127) Aggression in four and five year olds is usually related.

   A) People
   B) Possession
   C) Food
   D) Sleep

The correct answer is B:) Possession.

128) A parent who makes few demands on a child shows what parenting style?

   A) Permissive
   B) Authoritative
   C) Authoritarian
   D) Indulgent

The correct answer is A:) Permissive.

129) After a person moves to a new area they often hear airplanes flying overhead. After a month or two, they rarely notice them. What is this an example of?

   A) Auditory cliff
   B) Telegraphic speech
   C) Habituation
   D) Presbycusis

The correct answer is C:) Habituation.

130) Which of the following correctly orders the stages of dying?

   A) Anger, Denial, Bargaining, Acceptance, Depression
   B) Denial, Anger, Bargaining, Depression, Acceptance
   C) Bargaining, Denial, Anger, Depression, Acceptance
   D) Depression, Anger, Denial, Bargaining, Acceptance

The correct answer is B:) Denial, Anger, Bargaining, Depression, Acceptance. These stages were developed by Elisabeth Kubler-Ross.

131) The effects of regularly watching of the television program Sesame Street are positive only among

   A) Black children
   B) White children
   C) Lower income children
   D) No difference in race or economic status

The correct answer is D:) No difference in race or economic status.

132) Which sections of the brain are affected by Alzheimer's disease?

   A) Personality, hand eye coordination, and memory
   B) Memory, breathing, and speech
   C) Memory, speech, and personality
   D) Speech, personality, and breathing

The correct answer is C:) Memory, speech, and personality. Although all of the other answers identify two of the areas correctly, only answer C correctly identifies all three.

133) When someone assumes they will fail and do not even try to complete a task this is called

   A) Learned helplessness
   B) Negative effect
   C) Consequence
   D) Failure

The correct answer is A:) Learned helplessness.

134) According to Erikson's stages of development, older individuals are most likely to be concerned with which of the following?

   A) Guilt
   B) Trust
   C) Identify
   D) Integrity

The correct answer is D:) Integrity. The last of Erikson's eight stages is the older adult, or wisdom stage. The primary conflict in this stage is that of integrity vs. despair.

135) A parent who ignores a child's temper tantrum is hoping to discourage future tantrums by

Positive reinforcement
Negative reinforcement
C) Modeling
D) Extinction

The correct answer is D:) Extinction.

136) At approximately what age do children transfer from parallel play to associative play?

A) 1 year old
B) 2 years old
C) 3 years old
D) 4 years old

The correct answer is C:) 3 years old. At this age, children begin to share their toys and interact with one another, instead of engaging in parallel play.

137) Who coined the term modeling?

A) Freud
B) Piaget
C) Bandura
D) Erikson

The correct answer is C:) Bandura.

138) An individual with dyslexia will struggle with

A) Reading
B) Coloring
C) Sitting still
D) Forming friendships

The correct answer is A:) Reading. Dyslexia is a condition in which the brain has difficulty processing the written word. In some cases, dyslexia can also affect speech and writing skills.

139) Hypokinetic diseases are a result of

   A) Poor eating habits
   B) Insufficient exercise
   C) Genetics
   D) Poor hygiene

The correct answer is B:) Insufficient exercise. The word hypokinetic literally means "lack of movement." It is used to characterize diseases such as obesity, diabetes, and heart disease that arise often from a sustained lack of physical activity.

140) Which of the following is TRUE about convergent thinking?

   A) Convergent thinking is useful in fields such as math and science
   B) Creativity is an essential element of convergent thinking
   C) It is incredibility difficult to test convergent thinking using standardized methods
   D) Convergent thinking requires creativity

The correct answer is A:) Convergent thinking is useful in fields such as math and science. Convergent thinking is the ability to reason to a correct answer. It is also the easiest type of thinking to test using standardized methods because it is not subjective.

141) Which type of thinking relies most on creativity?

   A) Convergent thinking
   B) Diatomic thinking
   C) Rational thinking
   D) Divergent thinking

The correct answer is D:) Divergent thinking. Convergent thinking is the ability to use reason and information to come to a "correct" answer. Divergent thinking is the counterpart to it. It is the ability to think outside of the box and reach creative answers.

142) The dialectical perspective focuses on the existence of

    A) Pain
    B) Emotion
    C) Irrationalities
    D) Contradictions

The correct answer is D:) Contradictions. The dialectical perspective defines the world in terms of contradictions. The perspective seeks to reconcile contradictions through a process of reasoning to actual truth.

143) The amount of words spoken in a sentence is linked to

    A) Mean length of utterance
    B0 Echolalia
    C) Telegraphic speech
    D) Cooing

The correct answer is A:) Mean length of utterance.

144) According to Carol Gilligan, women are more likely to take which ethical perspective

    A) Justice
    B) Fairness
    C) Caring
    D) Logic

The correct answer is C:) Caring. Carol Gilligan developed the theory of ethics of care. She noted that women are more likely to take a perspective of ethics of care, whereas men are more likely to take a perspective of justice ethics. For this reason women are more nurturing and cooperative.

145) According to Erikson's theory of stages of development, which group of people are generally concerned with generativity vs self-absorption?

A) Infants
B) Adolescents
C) Young adults
D) Middle-aged adults

The correct answer is D:) Middle-aged adults. At this stage of development an individual will likely have settled down and started a career. Their main life focus is finding the balance between important things such as family, friends, and work, and ensuring that they maintain a strong sense of purpose and accomplishment.

146) What would a score of 7 on the Apgar scale indicate?

A) The baby is in critical condition and should see an expert immediately.
B) The baby requires some help to establish normal breathing.
C) Nothing can yet be determined, and the measurements should be taken again in two minutes.
D) The baby is well.

The correct answer is D:) The baby is well. The Apgar scale is a measure of heart rate, respiratory effort, muscle tone, color, and reflex irritability. The scale is from zero to ten with ten being the best.

 # Test Taking Strategies

Here are some test-taking strategies that are specific to this test and to other DSST tests in general:
- Keep your eyes on the time. Pay attention to how much time you have left.
- Read the entire question and read all the answers. Many questions are not as hard to answer as they may seem. Sometimes, a difficult sounding question really only is asking you how to read an accompanying chart. Chart and graph questions are on most DANTES/DSST tests and should be an easy free point.
- If you don't know the answer immediately, the new computer-based testing lets you mark questions and come back to them later if you have time.
- Read the wording carefully. Some words can give you hints to the right answer. There are no exceptions to an answer when there are words in the question such as always, all or none. If one of the answer choices includes most or some of the right answers, but not all, then that is not the answer. Here is an example:

> The primary colors include all of the following:
> A) Red, Yellow, Blue, Green
> B) Red, Green, Yellow
> C) Red, Orange, Yellow
> D) Red, Yellow, Blue

- Although item A includes all the right answers, it also includes an incorrect answer, making it incorrect. If you didn't read it carefully, were in a hurry, or didn't know the material well, you might fall for this.
- Make a guess on a question that you do not know the answer to. There is no penalty for an incorrect answer. Eliminate the answer choices that you know are incorrect. For example, this will let your guess be a 1 in 3 chance instead.

 # Test Preparation

How much you need to study depends on your knowledge of a subject area. If you are interested in literature, took it in school, or enjoy reading then your study and preparation for the literature or humanities test will not need to be as intensive as that of someone who is new to literature.

This book is much different than the regular DANTES study guides. This book actually teaches you the information that you need to know to pass the test. If you are particularly interested in an area, or feel that you want more information, do a quick search online. We've tried not to include too much depth in areas that are not as essential on the test. Everything in this book will be on the test. It is important to understand all major theories and concepts listed in the table of contents. It is also important to know any bolded words.

Don't worry if you do not understand or know a lot about the area. With minimal study, you can complete and pass the test.

To prepare for the test, make a series of goals. Determine a certain amount of time to review the information you have already studied and to learn additional material. Take notes as you study; it will help you learn the material.

Legal Note

All rights reserved. This Study Guide, Book and Flashcards are protected under the US Copyright Law. No part of this book or study guide or flashcards may be reproduced, distributed or stored in a retrieval system, or transmitted in any form or by any means, electronic, mechanical, photocopying, recording, or otherwise, without the prior written permission of the publisher Breely Crush Publishing, LLC.

References

[a] ATHERTON J S (2002) Learning and Teaching: Piaget's developmental psychology [On-line]: UK: Available: http://www.dmu.ac.uk/~jamesa/learning/piaget.htm Accessed: 28 March 2003, reprinted with permission.
[b] ATHERTON J S (2002) Learning and Teaching: Piaget's developmental psychology [On-line]: UK: Available: http://www.dmu.ac.uk/~jamesa/learning/piaget.htm Accessed: 28 March 2003, reprinted with permission.
[c] Young, Robert G., http://ryoung001.homestead.com/Freud.html Reprinted with permission.

FLASHCARDS

This section contains flashcards for you to use to further your understanding of the material and test yourself on important concepts, names or dates. Read the term or question then flip the page over to check the answer on the back. Keep in mind that this information may not be covered in the text of the study guide. Take your time to study the flashcards, you will need to know and understand these concepts to pass the test.

Wilhelm Wundt	**Francis Bacon**
Biological Approach	**Behavioral Approach**
Cognitive Approach	**Humanistic**
Psychoanalytical	**Structuralism**

Created scientific method	First scientific laborator
Study and observe behavior - blank slate	Personality is linked to genetics
All people are inherently good	How the mind learns and thinks
Classification of the minds structures	Actions are based on unconscious motivation

Functionalism	**Nature vs. Nurture**
Variable	**Constant**
Dependent Variable	**Independent Variable**
Correlational Research	**Clinical Psychologist**

Whether or not biology plays a part in personality	William James - the "how" part of behavior
A variable that always stays the same	A changing part of the person
The variables that the experimenter controls	The variable the experiment is trying to get information about
Doctoral degree in Psychology, cannot prescribe medicine	How much one variable changes in relation to each other

Psychiatrist	**Ethics**
Hypothalamus	**Autonomic Nervous System**
Sympathetic Nervous System	**Parasympathetic Nervous System**
Limbic System	**Hippocampus**

Principals and standards of behavior including morals	A medical doctor with a degree in Psychotherapy, can prescribe drugs
Involuntary system	Part of the endocrine system
Calming part of the system	Arousing part of the system
Stores memories	Memory and emotion center

Cerebral Cortex	**Occipital Lobe**
Temporal Lobe	**Frontal Lobe**
Parietal Lobe	**Cerebrum**
Cerebellum	**Pons**

Vision	Most developed and largest part of the brain
Voluntary muscles and intelligence	Hearing
The two large halves of the brain	Body sensations
Control breathing and heart rate	Coordinates all movements and muscles

Brain Stem	**Thalamus**
Hypothalamus	**Gregor Mendel**
Somatic Cell	**Cloning**
Gametes	**Zygote**

Main relay station for sensory signals	Sends commands to all other parts of the body
Father of genetics	Regulates internal temperature
Reproduction done with just the somatic cell	A full set of chromosomes
First part of a human	Reproductive cells (eggs and sperm)

Vestibular Sense	**Absolute Threshold**
Sclera	**Iris**
Pupil	**Cornea**
Lens	**Retina**

How much sensation one has to have to feel something	Balance and body movement
Colored part of the eye	White part of the eye
A clear membrane that protects the eye	Part of the eye that is black, opens and closes to let in light
Back of the eye. Contains rods and cones.	Transparent and located in front of the eye

Cones	**Noise**
Frequency	**Pitch**
Amplitude	**Loudness**
Timbre	**Outer Ear**

Irrelevant stimuli that competes for attention	Use to view color
Ear's interpretation of a sound's frequency	The number of full wavelengths that pass through a point in a given amount of time
A sound wave's amplitude	Amount of pressure produced by a sound wave and is measured in decibels
Includes pinna and external auditory canal	The perceptual quality of sound

Middle Ear

Inner Ear

Cochlea

Organ of Corti

Gestalt Psychology

Depth Perception

Visual Cliff

Erik Erickson

Oval window, cochlea, organ of Corti	Eardrum, anvil, stirrup
A part of the ear inside the cochlea	A fluid filled structure in thinner ear that looks like a snail
Makes people see objects in three dimensions	People organize their perceptions by patterns
Psychoanalyst	Proof that babies have depth perception

Most important thing to Erickson	**Trust vs. Mistrust**
Autonomy vs. Shame and Doubt	**Initiative vs. Guilt**
Industry vs. Inferiority	**Identity vs. Role Confusion**
Intimacy vs. Isolation	**Generativity vs. Stagnation**

| Infant | Development of trust |

| Preschooler | Toddler |

| Adolescent | School-Age |

| Middle-Age Adult | Young Adult |

Ego Integrity vs. Despair

Jean Piaget

Accommodation

Classificatio

Class Inclusion

Conservation

Developmental Norm

Egocentrism

Cognitive theorist	Old age
The ability to group objects together on a basis of common features	The difference made to one's mind or concepts by the process of assimilation
The realization that objects or sets of objects stay the same even when they are changed about or made to look different	The understanding of more advanced than simple classification, that someclasses or sets of objects are also sub-sets of a larger class
The belief that you are the center of the universe and everything revolves around you	A statistical measure of typical scores for categories of information

Elaboration	**Operation**
Recognition	**Recall**
Schema	**Stage**
Reflexive Stage (0-2 months)	**Primary Circular Reactions (2-4 months)**

The process of working something out in your head	Relating new information to something familiar
Being able to reproduce knowledge from memory	The ability to identify correctly something encountered before
A period in a child's development in which he or she is capable of understanding some things but not others	The representation in the mind of a set of perceptions, ideas, and/or actions, which go together
Reflexive behaviors occurin stereotyped repetition such as opening and closing fingers repetitivel	Simple reflex activity suchas grasping and sucking

Secondary Circular Reactions (4-8 months)	**Coordination of Secondary Reactions (8-12 months)**
Tertiary Circular Reactions (12-18 months)	**Invention of New Means Through Mental Combination (18-12 months)**
Preoperational Phase (2-4 years)	**Intuitive Phase (4-7 years)**
Period of Concrete Operations (7-11 years)	**Period of Formal Operation (11-15 years)**

Responses become coordinated into more complex sequences. Actions take on an "intentional" character.	Repetition of change actions to reproduce interesting consequences such as kicking one's feet to move a mobile suspended over the crib
Evidence of an internal representational system. Symbolizing the problem-solving sequence before actually responding. Deferred imitation.	Discovery of new ways to produce the same consequence or obtain the same goal such as the infant may pull a pillow toward him in an attempt to get a toy resting on it
Speech becomes more social, less egocentric. The child has an intuitive grasp of logical concepts in some areas.	Increased use of verbal representation but speech is egocentric. The beginnings of symbolic rather than simple motor play.
Though becomes more abstract, incorporating the principles of formal logic. The ability to generate abstract propositions, multiple hypotheses and their possible outcomes is evident.	Evidence for organized, logical thought. There is the ability to perform multiple classificationtasks, order objects in a logical sequence, and comprehend the principle of conservation.

Oral Stage	**Anal Stage**
Phallic Stage	**Latency Stage**
Genital Stage	**Denial**
Suppression	**Reaction Formation**

1-3 Years	Birth-1 year
6-11 Years	3-6 Years
Complete rejection of the feeling or situation	Adolescence
Turning a feeling into the exact opposite feeling. For example, saying you hate someone you are interested in.	Hiding the feelings and not acknowledging them

Projection	**Displacement**
Rationalization	**Regression**
Sublimation	**Self-actualization**
Esteem Needs	**Belonging and Love**

Feelings are redirected to someone else. Someone who has a bad day at work and can't complain goes home and yells at their kids instead.	Projection is transferring your thoughts and feelings onto others. For example, someone who is being unfaithful themselves constantly accuses their partner of cheating.
Reverting to old behavior to avoid feelings	You deny your feelings and come up with ways to justify your behavior
Highest need in hierarchy - Level 5	A type of displacement, redirection of the feeling into a socially productive activity
Level 3 need	Level 4 need

Safety	Physical Needs
Operant Conditioning	Instructional Conditioning
Extinction	Egocentric Behavior
Social Learning Theory	Baby Albert

Level 1 need	Level 2 need
Gives a negative sanction	Reinforces good behavior
A child does not take into consideration other people's needs	The process of unassociating the condition with the response
Was kept in a box and conditioned	Explicit role instruction (stereotypes), boys play with trucks and cars, girls wear make-up

Stimulus Generalization	**Naturalistic Observation**
Id	**Ego**
Super Ego	**Visual Cliff**
Object Permanence	**Harry Harlow**

Search conducted by watching the subject	Something from conditioning carries over to another related area
The mediator between ego and id	Primitive part of the subconscious which wants food and sex
Experiment to prove infants have depth perception	Ethical, super good part of the subconscious
Monkey experiment - monkeys liked the soft one better	Understanding that an object does not cease to exist once it has left your vision